# Women
# Religion
# Revolution

Edited by

Xochitl Alvizo and Gina Messina

Feminist Studies in Religion
FSR BOOKS

Published by Feminist Studies in Religion Books
A Unit of FSR, Inc.
Cambridge, MA
www.fsrinc.org

Produced by Dog Ear Publishing
4011 Vincennes Rd
Indianapolis, IN 46268
www.dogearpublishing.net

Cover image: © 2011 Arthur Loosley
"Revolutionary Graffiti"

ISBN: 978-1-4575-4639-6

This book is printed on acid-free paper.

Printed in the United States of America

*To our fearless feminist foresisters who continue to carry their torches and have courageously shared their flames to ignite ours. Especially Mary Daly and Rosemary Radford Ruether. And to our future foresisters, especially Sarah Messina-Dysert, a feminist revolutionary in training.*

# Contents

Acknowledgments      vii

Editors      ix

Contributors      xi

Foreword: Diving into the Wreck      xv

    *Carol J. Adams*

Introduction      1

1.   The Wound Is Where the Light Enters (and Emanates from) You      7

    *Jennifer Zobair*

2.   Birthing Revolution      15

    *Gina Messina*

3.   The Making of a Revolutionary      21

    *Amy Hoyt*

4.   The Alchemy of Survival      29

    *Edyka Chilomé*

5.   The Matter of Power: Organizing as Women of Faith of Color      35

    *Mollie Costello and Sandhya Jha*

6.   The Smallness of Radicalism      47

    *Kate McElwee*

7.  Mormon Feminism: Embracing Our Past, Envisioning Our Future                                                           53

    *Caroline Kline*

8.  Reproducing Justice                                                      59

    *Kate Ott*

9.  Pregnant with Sacred Truth                                               67

    *Katey Zeh*

10. Shamed Bodies: Eating, Empathy, and Sisterhood as Spiritual Practices of Revolt                                              75

    *Stephanie N. Arel*

11. Firsthand Experience with Secondhand Shopping                            85

    *Grace Y. Kao*

12. More Than Clothes Coming Off: Approaching Feminist Theology from the Strip Club                                         93

    *Betsy Coughlin*

13. Art As Spiritual Revolution                                             101

    *Angela Yarber*

14. Letting Go to Let God                                                   109

    *Rabia Chaudry*

15. Christ, the Cosmic Vagina: Fear, Power, and Connectedness in Feminist Religious Peacebuilding                              115

    *Trelawney Grenfell-Muir*

16. Losing My Tribalism (but Not My Tribe); Gaining the World                                                             127

    *Nurete Brenner*

17. I Dream Myself a Revolutionary                                          135

    *Xochitl Alvizo*

# Acknowledgments

All feminist projects are collaborative in nature; and thus, there are many with whom we must share our gratitude. First and foremost, we are so grateful to FSR Books for immediately recognizing the value of this project. To be welcomed among the first volumes published within this feminist series is truly an honor. In addition, we are extremely grateful to the Carter Center for its generous grant support of the FSR Books series toward publication of works that are consistent with the Carter Center's activities under its Human Rights Program and its Mobilizing Action for Women and Girls Initiative. (To learn more about the Center's Forum on Women, Religion, Violence, and Power, see http://forumonwomen.cartercenter.org/#.) We would also like to express our gratitude to Tony Damjanov and Tennille Ruth for their artistic design efforts and incredible skills, which allowed us to communicate the message and tone we hoped for in this anthology.

*Women Religion Revolution* is graced with the voices of so many brilliant feminists. Without their courage and strength, this volume would not exist. We are greatly appreciative to Carol Adams, who agreed to write the foreword. Her scholarship and activism represent the spirit of this anthology, and she is an exemplar for all feminist revolutionaries.

The community of feminists that we have the opportunity to engage and collaborate with is wide ranging and stretches around the globe. While it is impossible to name every person who has offered encouragement and support in a multitude of forms along the way, here we must acknowledge that it is this community that allows us all to press on and continue our work. Among this community are the amazing women and men of the Santa Barbara Feminist Writing Retreat who offered a supportive and safe space to bring this volume together. To all feminist revolutionaries, thank you for your unwavering commitment to transform this world in life-giving ways.

# *Editors*

**Xochitl Alvizo** loves all things feminist, womanist, and *mujerista*. She dedicates her work to bringing a feminist focus to theology and the study of religion, including feminist and queer theologies, congregational studies, and ecclesiology. Her work is inspired by the conviction that all people are inextricably connected and what we do, down to the smallest thing, matters. She is cofounder of Feminism and Religion and is cofounder of the Pub Church, Boston. She teaches in the area of women and religion, and the philosophy of sex, gender, and sexuality at California State University, Northridge.

**Gina Messina** earned her PhD at Claremont Graduate University. She is assistant professor of religion and gender studies at Ursuline College and cofounder of Feminism and Religion. She writes for the *Huffington Post*, has authored multiple publications, and most recently coedited the highly acclaimed *Faithfully Feminist: Jewish, Christian, and Muslim Feminists on Why We Stay* (2015). Messina is a widely sought after speaker and has presented across the United States at universities, organizations, and conferences, and on national platforms, including appearances on MSNBC, Tavis Smiley, NPR, and the TEDx stage. She has also spoken at the Commission on the Status of Women at the United Nations to discuss matters affecting the lives of women around the world. Messina is active in movements to end violence against women and explore opportunities for spiritual healing.

# Contributors

**Stephanie N. Arel** completed a PhD from Boston University's School of Theology and is currently a fellow at the Institute for the Bio-cultural Study of Religion at Boston University. She serves on the Intercontinental Academia on Human Dignity, hosted jointly by Hebrew University and Bielefeld University. Her research focuses on the impact of trauma, shame, and violence on human flourishing. She is the author of *Shame, Affect Theory, and Christian Formation* (2016) and coeditor with Shelly Rambo of a collection of essays entitled *Post-Traumatic Public Theology* (2016).

**Nurete Brenner** is an American Israeli who has been moving back and forth between the United States and Israel her entire life. Currently, she lives in Cleveland, Ohio, where she is executive director of the Business Unit and director of the Socially Conscious MBA program at Ursuline College. She received her PhD in organizational behavior from Case Western Reserve University, and her dissertation research was on Arab-Jewish dialogue groups throughout the United States. Nurete is also mother to two young boys whom she hopes will also always be comfortable moving between cultures, languages, and countries and who remind her on a daily basis of the importance of dialogue and social consciousness.

**Rabia Chaudry** is an attorney, Jennings Randolph Senior Fellow at the US Institute of Peace, International Security Fellow at New America, and a fellow of the Shalom Hartman Institute. She is the public advocate of

Adnan Syed, the wrongfully convicted man featured in podcast *Serial*, and is coproducer/host of the podcast *Undisclosed*. She is a frequent public speaker and writer, and author of *Adnan's Story* (2016).

**Mollie Costello** is an activist in Oakland, California. She is founder and director of the Alan Blueford Center for Justice.

**Betsy Coughlin** is a writer who studied at Boston University School of Theology. She lives in Nashville, Tennessee, where she explores spiritual care and hospital chaplaincy.

**Trelawney Grenfell-Muir** is an adjunct professor in the Department of Conflict Resolution, Human Security, and Global Governance with a specialization in cross-cultural conflict at the University of Massachusetts, Boston. She holds an MDiv from the Boston University School of Theology with a concentration in religion and conflict, and a PhD in conflict studies and religion with the University Professors Program at Boston University. She was a fellow at the Institute of Culture, Religion, and World Affairs and at the Earhart Foundation. Grenfell-Muir has conducted field research in situations of ongoing conflict in Syria, Lebanon, and Northern Ireland.

**Amy Hoyt** is a visiting assistant professor of religious studies at the University of the Pacific. Her research centers upon women, religion, and ethics. Her most recent work examines how religion influences women's experiences with reconciliation after national conflict.

**Grace Yia-Hei Kao** is associate professor of Ethics at Claremont School of Theology. Kao teaches and researches issues related to human and nonhuman animal rights, religion in the public sphere in the United States, ecofeminism, and Asian American Christianity. She has also published chapters and articles on the relationship between religion and violence and the issue of interreligious cooperation and conflict.

**Caroline Kline** is a PhD candidate in religion at Claremont Graduate University. Her areas of interest are Mormon women, gender theory, and theology. She is the coeditor of *Mormon Women Have Their Say: Essays from the Claremont Oral History Collection* (2013) and has been published in the journal *Feminist Theology*.

**Sandhya Jha** is the daughter of a mother from Scotland and a father from India. Jha serves as director of the Oakland Peace Center and as an antiracism trainer in the Christian Church (Disciples of Christ). She is an ordained minister and has a career in both parish and regional ministry as well as organizing and advocacy around housing justice and religious liberty issues. She also makes a really decent shrimp curry and loves to sing the blues. Her one true love is the town called Oakland.

**Kate McElwee** is coexecutive director of the Women's Ordination Conference and an elected leadership circle member of Women's Ordination Worldwide. McElwee is a respected feminist voice for women's equality in the Roman Catholic Church and is frequently featured in international media for her activism, grassroots organizing, and commentary. She earned her bachelor's in religion from Mount Holyoke College and a master's in international human rights law from the School of Oriental and African Studies (SOAS—University of London). McElwee lives and works in Rome, Italy, with her husband.

**Kate Ott** is a feminist, Catholic scholar addressing the formation of moral communities with specializations in sexuality, technology, children/youth, race, and professional ethics. She is assistant professor of Christian social ethics at Drew University Theological School and Drew's first Everyday Ethics Scholar. She is at work on a new book manuscript, currently titled "Life Enhancing Settings: The Technology and Ethics of Everyday Living." Her other books include *Sex + Faith: Talking with Your Child from Birth to Adolescence* (2013) and the coedited volume *Faith, Feminism, and Scholarship: The Next Generation* (2011). To find out more about her work visit www.kateott.org.

**Edyka Chilomé**, born Erica Granados–De La Rosa, is a queer woman of color cultural worker based in North Texas. She holds a BA in social and political philosophy from Loyola University Chicago and an MA in multicultural women's studies from Texas Women's University, where her research focused on the decolonial power of spiritual [Art]ivism. Granados–De La Rosa has been asked to share her poetry and speak on social justice issues around the country and in Latin America. She currently serves as a faculty member of the presidential award-winning initiative, The Clemente Course for the Humanities at El Centro College in Dallas, Texas.

**Angela Yarber** is an author, artist, and activist with a PhD in art and religion from the Graduate Theological Union. The author of seven books that address the intersections among the arts, religion, and gender/sexuality, she is also the recipient of three awards for Top LGBTQ Christian Books. Currently, Yarber is a part-time assistant professor of women's, gender, and sexuality studies at Wake Forest University and creator of the Holy Women Icons Project. For more on her work, or to purchase an icon, visit www.angelayarber.com.

**Katey Zeh**, MDiv is a thought leader, strategist, and writer at the intersections of faith and reproductive health. She is currently working on a book entitled "Women Rising" that connects the lives of biblical women with today's global movements for gender justice. Zeh is a graduate of Davidson College and Yale Divinity School. She lives in Cary, NC, with her husband Matt and their daughter Samantha.

**Jennifer Zobair** is a graduate of Smith College and Georgetown University Law Center. She is author of the debut novel, *Painted Hands* (2013), and coeditor of *Faithfully Feminist: Jewish, Christian, and Muslim Feminists on Why We Stay* (2015). She has written and spoken widely about the intersection of gender and religion. More information about her work can be found on her website at www.jennifer-zobair.com.

# FOREWORD:

## *Diving into the Wreck*

During the early 1990s, I worked on a book, *Woman-Battering*, for Fortress Press's Creative Pastoral Care and Counseling Series. Before handing in the manuscript, I gave it to a professor of pastoral care for review. Several weeks later, we sat down to talk about it. He felt the advice was helpful, accurate, and practical. He pointed out some places where the language could be clearer. Then he told me the manuscript contained one main problem.

I remember how he leaned across his desk toward me, saying, "Carol, the problem is you assume that just because a minister *knows* the right thing to do, he'll *do* it." (The professor used "he.") Meeting my puzzled look, he explained that some ministers are inherently passive individuals; they *know* the right thing to do; yet, they do not do it. They might sit in their chairs, listening to a battered woman describe what happened to her, and know what to instruct her, yet not act, not provide guidance on possible steps she could take for safety. Furthermore, when a batterer sat in front of them, knowing what they should do, they would be unable to hold that individual accountable or act in an appropriate way that the urgency of the situation required.

I never imagined such passivity: that someone in ministry might *know* the right thing to do and yet be unable to act in a way congruent to that knowledge! *Women Religion Revolution* gathers the stories of women who understand that passivity is not an option. Each essay thrums with the story of an embodied, articulate, passionate woman who emerges from her own experience to make connections. The congruence of life and vision, of activism and theory, sings through these pages.

Some of the essays remind us of the confusion that besets us when we experience oppression: atomized within our own experience of it, deprived of connections, we begin to walk a path that seemingly has not yet been traversed. Date rape, sexual abuse, domestic violence, addictions, and other experiences isolate. But soon we find that our paths seeking healing and transformation lead us toward others.

During the 1974–75 academic year, I participated in an amazing course at Harvard Divinity School, a feminist metahistory course taught by Clarissa (Chrissy) Atkinson. (Yes, as Xochitl Alvizo's essay suggests at its beginning, the early 1970s remain an example of revelatory and amazing times.) The Harvard course and our questions during that year took their inspiration from Adrienne Rich's poem "Diving into the Wreck." In that poem, Rich describes how, after reading "the book of myths," the narrator goes in search of "the wreck and not the story of the wreck / the thing itself and not the myth."[1]

Our approach to history was the radical one of questioning the religious myths in Western history: Whose story was it? Who was telling the story? How did the story differ from the records that remained? It was a heady, exciting year. Each of us took turns making presentations. Emily Culpepper, whose short film *Period Piece* brought the discussion of menstruation into the domain of theology, presented her further research on the issue.[2] Diane Miller, who was reconstructing the stories of nineteenth-century Unitarian and Universalist

---

[1] Adrienne Rich, "The Wreck," *Diving into the Wreck: Poems 1971–1972* (New York: Norton, 1973), https://www.poets.org/poetsorg/poem/diving-wreck.

[2] Emily Erwin Culpepper, Gannit Ankori, Karen L. King, Sarah K. Peck, and Claudia Ann Highbaugh, "Positively Breaking Taboos: Why and How I Made the Film *Period Piece*," and responses, *Journal of Feminist Studies in Religion* 22, no. 2 (Fall 2006): 125–53.

women ministers, described how she enlisted women who were members of the Midwestern churches these women had served a century earlier to help with the research.[3] And it was there that I presented my first ideas on feminism and vegetarianism that eventually became *The Sexual Politics of Meat*.

Diving into the wreck means we understand there is a *wreck*, something we need to see and probe. The wreck, in one sense, is oppression in its many manifold expressions. It is who has been left out and why. It is what we have experienced and what it means. It is multiple voices articulating their experience. The women in this anthology dive into the wreck and eloquently describe what they find there. We are diving into the wreck not to rebuild it but to know it.

With other feminist scholars, I have worked on identifying and articulating key aspects of a feminist care ethics. Simone Weil, a twentieth-century French mystic and writer, famously said, "the love of our neighbor in all its fullness simply means being able to say, 'What are you going through?'" She suggests that this is the task of *attention*—asking our neighbors, "What are you going through?" and being willing to listen for an answer. She writes that this question is a recognition that the sufferer exists "not as a unit in a collection, or a specimen from the social category labeled 'unfortunate,'" but as an individual who "was one day stamped with a special mark by affliction." This way of looking is "first of all attentive. The soul empties itself of all its own contents in order to receive into itself the being it is looking at, just as he is, in all his truth."[4]

Attentiveness is a political act. It is listening to those who have been seemingly deemed of no importance, and announcing, "You are important. You are a beloved individual." This volume calls us to

---

[3] Diane offered slide shows, talks, and an exhibit. The exhibit, done jointly with Reverend Denise Tracy, is now accessioned by the Andover-Harvard library at Harvard Divinity School, titled "American Herstory: A Documentary Exhibit of Our American Foremothers," 1975–76.

[4] Simone Weil, "Reflections on the Right Use of School Studies," in *Waiting on God*, trans. Emma Crawford (1971; repr., London: Routledge and Kegan Paul, 1951), 75. Josephine Donovan and I draw on Weil in our writings on *The Feminist Care Tradition in Animal Ethics* (New York: Columbia University Press, 2007).

listen in a strip club or at an abortion clinic or hospital eating disorder unit or a domestic violence shelter. It calls us to listen while community organizing in Oakland, while working for women's ordination, or while blogging collectively or teaching. It tells of listening in Nairobi or at Pub Church or in a Jewish-Arab dialogue group. What the contributors to this volume know is that attentiveness is revolutionary and the opposite of passivity.

Caring and listening are political acts. Nelle Morton revolutionized our understanding of consciousness-raising groups of the early 1970s by defining them as places where we heard others into speech. She wrote, "there is no doubt that when a group of women hear another woman to speech, a presence is experienced in the new speech."[5] Certainly, the Harvard course heard us into radical and revelatory speech. As I think back to that ovular (no seminar for us!), I remember women hearing each other into questioning the accepted interpretations. What emerged was radical scholarship. There we were nurtured intellectually and emotionally. One has the sense that the women whose voices are gathered here similarly experienced being heard into speech and likewise hear others into speech.

This work is so much easier when we are connected to others. I know it was the Boston-Cambridge feminist community, with teachers like Mary Daly and Chrissy Atkinson, that heard me into speech about how patriarchal ethics installs eating animals as one aspect of culture. I realized that we can ask of the other animals, "What are you going through," and they offer answers—nonverbal to be sure, yet answers all the same. They are suffering; they are lonely; they are in pain; they have lost their children; they want to escape.

In the following essays, we learn the specifics of what prophetic women have been going through, and they also point us to ways in which we can actively be involved in asking others, "What are you going through?" One recurring message is that we do not need to do this alone, not anymore. Part of our work is to resist isolation, refuse it, and allow for connections. Connections can be lifesaving. We can

---

[5] Nelle Morton, *The Journey Is Home* (Boston: Beacon, 1985), 127–28.

respond to and shape a faith that is responsive and revelatory to our most urgent questions and that challenges oppression.

How do we live the revolution? Pull up a chair, and listen. And then ask, "What, now, is my next step? What, now, is my understanding of revolution and resistance and revelation?" Good, let us, together, go forward.

Carol J. Adams

# Introduction

In a world where women's issues are political issues, feminism and religion are incorrectly scripted as opposing sides. Drawing on the messages of love and social justice from within their religious traditions, women are leading feminist movements that promote positive social change at both micro and macro levels. The authors in this volume show how religion is fueling women's efforts to revolutionize the world. The stories collected here call us to recognize these revolutions and to go forth with renewed courage and boldness.

Looking back through US history, religion and feminism have had a long partnership. During the first wave of feminism, abolition and women's suffrage were only one part of a larger social reform effort that drew on religious values. Seeking liberation, women challenged biblical teachings that were interpreted as ordaining marginalization and enslavement and focused on the liberative message of the Gospels in demanding basic human rights. The women's liberation movement of the late sixties and early seventies was a distinct time of revolutionary activism of large-scale proportions in the United States that quickly led to feminist critiques and reconstructions of patriarchal religion. The work of Mary Daly, Rosemary Radford Ruether, Delores Williams, Audre Lorde, Chung Hyun Kyung, Ada María Isasi-Díaz, Judith Plaskow, and Carol Christ resulted in a new dialogue about women's roles, as well as racial and gender biases in religious traditions.[1] Early criticisms regarding racial inclusion within feminist movements likewise challenged women to do their own internal work. Such revolutionary activism continues today, often on a large scale thanks to the online feminist movement.

This said, today, many of the revolutions women are leading have a more localized expression as they continue the important work still needed to create a socially just society. The revolution we are focused on in this volume is not a revolution writ large in which the aim is to topple state governments, nor may it have the impact of changing the discipline of religious studies as was the case with the feminist theology that grew out of the women's liberation movement in the eighties and early nineties. It is focused on the persistent and faithful work that most often happens on a small scale every day in women's lives and contributes in dismantling oppressive systems of injustice and harm at every level, at times starting with those embedded in our own religious traditions. This revolution occurs in various ways with different strategies, from disrupting norms in the home to launching organized efforts that challenge oppressive structures within religion.

For centuries people have tried and tried again to create change, to "free the masses," to save people from suffering, misery, and oppression—but too often revolutionaries resort to violence as their means. The systems in place are so stubborn and rigid that the revolutionary comes to see no other way to bring about radical social change except through a widespread violent overthrow. But this form of revolution

---

[1] Mary Daly's *The Church and the Second Sex*, first published in 1968, was a foundational text that interwove the feminist ideology of Simone de Beauvoir with problematic doctrine to reveal the inherit sexism within Christian dogma. Rosemary Radford Ruether's *Sexism and God Talk: Toward a Feminist Theology* (Boston: Beacon Press, 1983) has become a feminist classic in addressing "misinterpretations" of tradition and offering new constructions of dogma that honor the full humanity of women. Delores S. Williams' *Sisters in the Wilderness: The Challenge of Womanist God-Talk* (Maryknoll, NY: Orbis, 1993) brought black women's experience specifically to bear on biblical interpretation. Audre Lorde's "Open Letter to Mary Daly" (September 22, 1979, https://feminismandreligion.files.wordpress.com/2011/10/mary-daly-to-audre-lorde00012.pdf) "ignited public conversations about embedded racism found in feminist theology."

comes at the cost of people's freedom and well-being. It silences dissenting voices, suppresses alternative visions, and stifles creativity and difference for the sake of effectiveness of achieving "the cause." A revolution that takes away human freedom and creativity is no revolution at all. It fails to go deep enough, fails to get at the roots that must be engaged to bring about the radical change that responds to the cries against injustice that come from "deep within the human heart."[2]

Gerard Lohfink is a Catholic theologian who has written extensively on the role of church in the transformation of the world. While his context and subject is Christian, specifically Catholic, his reflections regarding the importance of small communities of faith as the place where God begins Her revolutionary work can be extended to apply to the contexts women in this book write about and the social justice activism in which they participate. Lohfink posits how God would start a revolution that still respects human freedom and participation, stating:

> God, like all revolutionaries, desires the overturning, the radical alteration of the whole society—for in this the revolutionaries are right: what is at stake is the whole world, and the change must be radical, for the misery of the world cries to heaven and it begins deep within the human heart. But how can anyone change the world and society at its roots without taking away freedom?

> It can only be that God begins in a small way, at one single place in the world. There must be a place, visible, tangible, where the salvation of the world can begin: that is, where the world becomes what it is supposed to be . . . Everyone must have the opportunity to come and see. All must have the chance to behold and test this new thing. Then if they want to, they can allow themselves to be drawn into the

---

[2] Gerhard Lohfink, *Does God Need the Church? Toward a Theology of the People of God* (Wilmington, DE: Michael Glazier, 1999), 27.

history of salvation that God is creating. Only in that way can their freedom be preserved. What drives them to the new thing cannot be force, not even moral pressure, but only the fascination of a world that is changed.[3]

That vision, in which the transformation of the world begins in small, contextual, tangible ways, makes sense for a revolution that values the freedom and dignity of all human persons. The stories in this book help capture the fascination of a world that is changed. They call us to imagine the particular beautiful part of the revolution we are part of in our own communities, with our friends, family, and neighbors, in our particular time and place. We participate in the incarnation, the embodiment of a divine new reality that begins within us and is shared and worked out in participation with others in a particular, tangible place . . . we are, as Carol Christ states, cocreators with Goddess, inspired to live "creatively, joyfully, and in harmony with others in the web of life."[4] This is a transformed world indeed!

Tremendous widespread transformations, as they relate to systemic and institutional oppression and injustice, must also take place. Systemic injustices must be collectively resisted, protested, interrupted, and dismantled. However, they cannot be simply replaced with an alternate system or institution that supposedly works at all times for all people in all places—that is a patriarchal fallacy. Particularity matters. Context, creativity, and participation always have a place. Human freedom and dignity cannot be sacrificed—otherwise, the "new thing" will not be new at all. The roots will still be rotten.

The world indeed needs overturning. We stand with radical feminist ideology here—the change must be radical, for the whole world is at stake. The change must start from deep within the roots if a truly new creation is to be brought to life. But it is our contention that the overturning cannot, *will not*, occur if done in the same old domineering, violent form that imposes a single grand vision onto all people.

---

3 Ibid.
4 Carol P. Christ, "She Who Changes," *Feminism and Religion*. May 21, 2012, https://feminismandreligion.com/2012/05/21/she-who-changes-by-carol-p-christ/.

Sonia Johnson rightly affirms that "what we are doing in the present is creating the future, *is* the future."[5] In other words, the means are the ends, and *how* we do something *is* what we get. The radical change initiated by the Divine starts with us, within us, and engages us as free and creative beings, cultivating in us the very transformation toward which we move. As we and the communities of which we are a part begin to transform into and embody beautiful, just, life-giving, and new ways, others will have the chance to behold and test the new thing, to be drawn into it out of sheer fascination—fascination that a new thing is not just possible but is *made real*, and that the roots of change emerge in diverse and creative ways in every new time and in every new place.

So, how does the Divine change the world? It can only be that She begins in a small way at a single place in the world. It can only be that She begins with us. And that is precisely what the women in this book reveal.

As Emilie Townes so eloquently explains, to be able to question the "radical nature of oppression and devaluation of the self and the community in the context of structural evil" is to love one's heart . . .

> [it] requires that we be willing to confront—to face together. To take the risk of learning about the weak spots and places we need to work on as well as the riches within us . . . to face our own lack of understanding, the stereotypes we have within us, our unwillingness to change, our comfort with the status quo. It also means that we draw on our faith, the ability we have to hope, our unwillingness to let go of loving, and our accepting responsibility to do justice. . . . We are the harvest, we are each other's tomorrows, todays, and yesterdays.[6]

---

[5] Sonia Johnson, *Wildfire: Igniting the She/volution* (Albuquerque, NM: Wildfire, 1989), 38.

[6] Emilie M. Townes, "Washed in the Grace of God," in *Violence against Women and Children: A Christian Theological Sourcebook* (New York, NY: Continuum, 1995), 61.

Revolution begins with us.

Paying homage to foresisters who have paved the way, the next generation of feminist religious activists is heeding Towne's words, accepting their responsibility to do justice, picking up the torch, and continuing the struggle for radical change based on dignity and equity for all. From movements focused on reproductive justice to women's ordination to sustainable living, women are drawing from their religious foundations to inspire revolutions of social justice that call for transformative action in the world.

The stories shared in this book are of women participating in overturning oppressive systems and calling forth the transformation of the world while still respecting human freedom and dignity. They report on revolutionary work that is context specific, birthed from their experiences, concrete, tangible, small, but nonetheless radical in scope. They give witness to the resources for love and justice that varied religious traditions provide for this work. The women in this book, by sharing their stories and sparking our imaginations, invite us to reflect on the work of love and justice that we are called to do, and to be renewed by our collective courage and boldness. The revolution begins with us.

# CHAPTER 1

## The Wound Is Where the Light Enters (and Emanates from) You
### Jennifer Zobair

*This place where you are right now*
*God circled on a map for you.*
*Wherever your eyes and arms and heart can move*
*Against the earth and the sky,*
*The Beloved has bowed there—*
*Our Beloved has bowed there knowing*
*You were coming*

— Hafiz, "The Place Where You Are Right Now"

In my second year of law school, miserable, restless, I sat on the edge of the Dupont Circle fountain in front of the nude figures symbolizing the wind and the stars and the sea, and told a friend I didn't want to "do this" anymore—that I didn't want to be in law school or become a lawyer. He shrugged and said, "So don't." I tried to inflate those two words. I tried to make them large enough to confer permission, both to leave law school and to write. My friend knew something catastrophic had happened to me, and that of all the ways I tried to keep it from erasing me, only writing helped.

"It's okay to go," he said gently.

I nodded, but I lacked courage. And in the end, swimming in the expectations of friends, family, and student loan providers, I stayed.

Writing felt like an indulgence. Law, on the other hand, was the practical choice, the obvious way to both earn a living and fight for causes I was deeply committed to, like gender equality and racial justice. It would be years before I would encounter the work of Rumi, one of Islam's most beloved mystics, years before I would understand his words: "The wound is where the light enters you."[1] And so in that moment, on the edge of that fountain, I had no way of knowing that writing would become both my own lifeline, and the way I would ultimately try to throw one to others.

When people ask why I converted to Islam, it's easy to say "for marriage"—and it's also true. After law school, I met and married a Muslim man, and converted. But that singular narrative ignores all of the less obviously linear arcs of my story: the fact that I had a beloved Muslim friend in college who was so kind that being with her felt like a refuge. That I had spent years struggling as a Catholic feminist, and that I'd never fully grasped the concept of the Trinity. That I'd been assaulted the year before I met my husband.

A simple "for marriage" explanation also rather blithely glosses over the fact that it is one thing to study a religion or read a religious text, and quite another to join a religious community in all its particularity.

Which is to say, there are boxes for women. They can vary by culture or religion or class, but there are always boxes, and I have felt pressed into them. After I converted, the boxes became more oppressive and minimizing. In Surah 33:34, the Qur'an explicitly promises forgiveness and reward for believing men *and* women—an egalitarian

---

[1] Jalal al-Din Rumi, *The Essential Rumi*, new expanded ed., trans. Coleman Barks (New York: HarperCollins, 1995), 142.

point emphasized by the repetition of the word *women* ten times. Still, in practice, there seemed to be little parity between the social and religious status of Muslim men and women. My gender was separated. My body felt policed. My past felt judged. I sat silently and listened to Muslims imply or actually state that rape was the fault of Western women who drank or dressed inappropriately. For nearly two decades, I told only a single, solitary Muslim—my husband— that I was the survivor of a date rape. I wore my shame behind a mask. I kept my own secret for years.

In this and other ways, I buried my feminist self. And I knew that if I couldn't advocate for myself, I had no business being part of any larger movement or revolution for gender justice. In the hierarchy of miseries, the time I sat on the edge of the fountain in Dupont Circle, rethinking law school, took on the characteristics of a better time.

My mother loves to tell the story of how I once turned to her in church and asked why we said "Amen" instead of "Awomen." I was three years old. I believe it is in my DNA to know that once a woman understands her fundamental equality, that conviction can never be extinguished. Even if she's later marginalized or made to feel small, she will always find her way back to an empowered equilibrium. And so, after a few years in my new faith, I knew that I would either find exegeses that affirmed my full humanity or I would, for the second time in my life, leave my religion.

I sought out and read the work of pro-woman Muslim scholars like Leila Ahmed, Fatima Mernissi, amina wadud, and Asma Barlas. I inhaled everything I could get my hands on and sank with profound relief into the logic and persuasion of their work. This is what I had been looking for. This was a feminist theology that, much as it might surprise many non-Muslims, made more sense to me than the Catholic feminism I had struggled with years before.

But after epiphany came bewilderment. Why, I wondered, if scripture could be interpreted in ways that honored a woman's full humanity, would anyone—and especially *women*—choose to interpret it otherwise? And what would happen to stereotypes surrounding

Islam and women if non-Muslims knew there were compelling pro-woman interpretations of the Qur'an?

I felt inspired to join the struggle. I could write. I could use my voice. But soon after the flame was lit in my Muslim feminist self, terrorists who also called themselves Muslim flew planes into the Twin Towers and the Pentagon, killing thousands of innocent people. This country became fixated on Muslims, and rarely in positive ways. Suddenly, the worst "other" identity you could claim in America was Muslim.

How could I speak out about gender injustice in Muslim religious spheres without piling on—without playing in to every awful stereotype that the American public seemed so ready to embrace? For those who believe, the Qur'an has a powerful answer: "We have created you from male and female and made you peoples and tribes that you may know one another" (Surah 49:13).

That one divine sentence embodies such enormous and hopeful beauty. The idea that our differences—our diverse gender, religious, and racial identities—are *purposeful* is there for any believer who bothers to pay attention. It's lost on so many people and yet confirms what many of us have experienced: There is benefit in interacting with and caring about people who are not the same as we are. It expands our perspective. It forces us to step outside of ego and our limited ways of being. It allows us to see sameness in difference and to honor the ways we diverge. The writer in me, who revels in word choice, loves it in this verse, too. "Knowing" is not simply tolerating. Knowing requires me to do some work. It means you're worth some effort. It opens up the possibility of loving you.

In contrast, not "knowing" others can have harmful consequences. I have seen firsthand how stereotypes and bigotry hurt Muslims—men and women. I have also witnessed the substantive harm of sexism within the Muslim community. These are two sides of the same coin. They isolate. They create fear that leads to mistreatment. They deny our full humanity.

We are supposed to know each other. And the only way I have ever known to explain myself or my gender or my religion is to write.

I started with a novel. I told the fictional story of smart, success-ful Muslim women living and working in Boston. If you took away their religious identity, my novel would read like many other women's novels, and on one level, I wanted it to read that way. I wanted to let it be just a story, like so many other stories. But for two audiences, this story is unthinkable: non-Muslims do not believe women like my characters exist, and very conservative Muslims don't think they should. These are two harms of erasure driven by similar impulses, and I knew that on some level I was speaking to both.

I began to write more directly about these issues, penning essays and op-eds on feminism and religion. Eventually, I circled back to the young woman sitting on the edge of the Dupont Circle fountain and the catastrophic thing that threatened to erase her. I had tried to bury my rape for years. I insisted I was not going to write about it, nor would I out myself as a survivor to my fellow Muslims. But then I read an arti-cle about Syrian refugee women who had been raped but refused to tell relief workers what had happened to them. Because they felt shame in their conservative Muslim communities, they weren't getting help. I tried to tell myself none of this had anything to do with me, but the stories of those women sat like granite on my chest.

So, too, did the words of the brilliant Muslim feminist theolo-gian amina wadud: "One cannot stand on the sidelines in the face of injustice and still be recognized as fully Muslim, fully *khalifah.*"[2]

If a Muslim woman like me, who lives in a fairly liberal society, could not speak out about what happened to her, how could Syrian women in a conservative society get the help they needed? For Mus-lim women to have any hope of gender justice, at a very minimum we must be able to speak about sexual violence without shame or fear of sharia-based legal punishment.

It was time for me to get off the sidelines.

I wrote an essay about my own rape. I'm sure it did not change a single thing for women in Syria. But when it was published, other

---

[2] Amina Wadud, *Qur'an and Woman* (New York: Oxford University Press, 1999), xix.

women—and one man—wrote to me to tell me about their own sexual assaults: raw, heartbreaking stories that made me cry as I read them. Some of those who contacted me were Muslim women, and some of them said I was the only person they had ever told.

The cure for the pain, according to Rumi, is found in the pain, and I know this to be true.

Many brilliant and bold Muslim women are using their voices and talents to advocate for our rights and to insist on our full humanity. Still, as a convert, sometimes I struggle to find my place in that movement. It is perhaps no accident that one of my novel's main characters, Zainab Mir, tells a friend she is frustrated with the non-Muslims who stereotype her and the Muslims who attack her feminism. She says she is tired of both groups. The friend tells her she is carving out a third space and that this is difficult work.

"Revolution is a lonely thing, Zainab," she says.[3]

And sometimes it is. And sometimes it must be done anyway—and urgently—and sometimes it leads you to incredible people, like the women with whom you will work on an anthology, amazingly, *perfectly*, about feminism and religion. And sometimes you'll realize you can find revolutionary community in unlikely places, like in the warmest, gutsiest, most larger-than-life Catholic woman you've ever met, who will turn out to be your coeditor and later your friend.

And so I know other words of Rumi's are true as well—that when you start to walk on the way, the way appears.

Even though I ultimately became a writer, I don't regret going to law school, or those early years I practiced law. And I can't fully regret the time I spent navigating a conservative religious culture that did not fit me, uplift my spirit, or bring me closer to God. It shaped me. It has all formed the person I am today and, in turn, informed my activism. It brought me to this exact place that, according to the Sufi poet Hafiz, God circled on a map for me. And in this spot, in this very

[3] Jennifer Zobair, *Painted Hands* (New York: St. Martin's Press, 2013), 294.

moment, I cannot help but think of my favorite architect, who happens to be my brother, and the studio professor's advice he once shared with me: sometimes, you have to make a drawing to figure out what you want to draw.

*Exactly*, I think, and whisper it to the young woman sitting by the fountain.

# CHAPTER 2

## *Birthing Revolution*

### Gina Messina

B irthing. The process of giving birth. Of giving life. The emergence of young from a mother's womb. Birthing. As a woman, I had always understood this as my role, my duty, my responsibility. It is what I had learned from my church, education, family, and community. Women become mothers, raise children, and serve God through rearing new Catholic life. I had accepted and embraced this role; I was excited for it. I believed in the fairy tale. I would get married, have children, and live happily ever after. But then, like a dark looming cloud, it crept in and snuffed out my fairy tale. Infertility.

We generally do not think about infertility. It is something that happens to others; it is not expected. In fact, we often spend so much time trying not to get pregnant that it never occurs to us that getting pregnant is actually a feat for many. And for some an impossibility. Nor do we realize how rampant infertility is or how devastating its consequences.

As a newlywed at the young age of twenty-five, my first priority was to become a mother. I left it in "God's hands." I thought that when it was time, it would happen. God would know when I was ready. Then a year passed. Then two and three. And then, in year four, I wondered what God was waiting for and sought help.

I vividly remember sitting in my doctor's office. Looking at the images of the uterus encircling the fetus and the birth canal. I knew it was my path to be a mother; my "destiny." I held my hands across my womb. I could almost feel a child within, movement, a kick, a child birthing from my body. And then . . . that word . . . *infertility* . . . its weight, crushing.

A woman's value is in her womb, I was taught, and like so many of the women in the Bible, mine was barren. For quite some time I questioned my value. Theological teachings dictate that men and women have distinct but complementing roles. Complementarity, as dictated by the Catholic Church and reinforced by Pope Francis as "an anthropological fact," claims that women's primary responsibility is motherhood. We are to be Mary-like; to accept God's call to carry and give birth to children without question. And so, I wondered, if I could not fulfill such a role, what value did I have?

My barren state fueled resentment for the Catholic Church and I cursed God; *HE* had forsaken me. Only a male god would demand a woman bear such a cross.

I was trapped in a ritualistic cycle of grief. The first sight of blood became a symbolic death. Once again, the child I had prayed for was denied and I grieved. I wept, cursed God, and appealed to my biblical foremothers who shared in my barren state. I reflected on Sarah's anguish and her bitterness toward Hagar, her Egyptian hand-maiden who gave her husband an heir (Gen 16).[1] Rachel's envy became my envy. As she resented her sister who gave birth to seven children for the husband they shared (Gen 29), I also resented my sisters whose wombs had already been opened. However, once my blood flow ceased, I turned to the hope of Hannah whose "womb was closed by the Lord" (1 Gen 1:5); and yet she continued to pray for a son with hope that she would not be forgotten (1 Sam 1). I, too, pleaded with God to remember me and was filled with hope that my womb might be opened.

Nonetheless, Hannah's hope failed me. After 136 failed cycles, I claimed agency and decided that I would no longer leave ability to be

---

[1] For a critical analysis of race and privilege as it relates to Sarah's poor treatment of Hagar, see Williams, *Sisters in the Wilderness*.

a mother in "God's hands"; my child did not have to grow in my womb. I became a foster parent with the intent to adopt, and just three weeks after being added to the waiting list, my beautiful daughter came home to me. Finally, my prayers had been answered. At least so I thought—until three months later, when my child was taken away. The court ruled she had been placed with me in error and should have gone to a biological relative. The pain was unbearable. God was playing some kind of sick game with my life, and I no longer wanted to participate. I felt abused, shattered, empty.

In the midst of this acute tragedy, I somehow found the where-withal to put back together at least some parts of me and sought a way to move forward. It was the women in my life and feminist ideology that allowed me to move beyond my grief and reclaim my value and purpose. I followed an impulse to turn to my feminist sisters and embark on an intellectual, spiritual, and communal endeavor that I could love, nurture, and watch grow. FeminismandReligion.com (FAR)—a blogging project I cofounded with my partner in feminism (and this volume) Xochitl Alvizo and our feminist sisters Caroline Kline and Cynthia Garrity Bond—became that endeavor. This collaborative effort allowed me finally to achieve the birthing I so desired, and it was revolutionary.

FAR allowed me to "mother." In a time when I was desperate to nurture life, this project enabled me to participate in shaping something meaningful, and to do so in the company of my comothers. For me, FAR became a home. A place where I could express myself freely and engage in feminist dialogue in a way I often could not (and cannot) in other spaces. I developed relationships I would not have otherwise—relationships that have become the most life-giving and lifesaving. My feminist friendships span across the globe and these are women I love, trust, and can reach out to in an instant. My strongest relationships were developed in this online space. They were my family and became my salvation.

Six months after the founding of FAR, my daughter was returned to me, and my "traditional" family was resurrected. My beautiful child, now thirty months old, walked back into my arms, and I have never let her go. I know deep in my soul that she was meant for me, and I for her. And although she did not grow in my womb, she grew in my heart. I could have no greater love than what I have for my daughter. She is sassy, kind, loving, empathetic, and of course, a budding feminist. She is like her mom, and I am like her.

I will not deny that "traditional" motherhood is a revolution all on its own. It is necessary for me to acknowledge here the incredible revolutions launched every day by women who are raising families and living out traditional motherhood. I refuse to engage the "mommy wars"; all of our efforts count equally, and revolution occurs as a result. It is my great hope that every mother of all births recognizes the ways that she participates in positive social change; that she is a revolutionary.

At the same time, I also affirm that mothering comes to us in so many different ways, and each is important and should be celebrated. We become so bogged down in traditionalism, it is easy to lose ourselves and become blind to the many ways we achieve roles that do not fit the mold. It was through FAR that I regained a sense of my life having meaning regardless of my womb's status. And so my journey with FAR continues to be critical for so many reasons. For me, it is where my own revolution began. My ongoing struggle with infertility and brief separation from my daughter—as painful as it was—allowed me to fully understand who I am and the many ways my life as a woman has value.

FAR has grown and become an important resource for feminist conversations around religion and theology. Because of the benefits of technology, it has created a platform from which feminists across the globe can share their views and engage in thoughtful dialogue about pressing issues; a space where women and men in 181 countries find voice. So many of us are silenced in our religious communities; projects like FAR and other social media platforms offer an opportunity to vocalize our thoughts, to break through imposed borders, and to reclaim our power. As a result, FAR has expanded borders and created new frontiers. FAR has become its own revolution.

Every revolution—every micro or macro *turn* that brings about justice and human flourishing—is of the utmost importance in the movement for a more just society. As I reflect on my research, writing, teaching, and co-birthing of FAR, I see that I have birthed a revolution based in love, justice, and faith, on the foundation of Catholic social teaching. If we can each recognize the multiple meanings of birthing and the many ways we participate in creating new life, while comprehending what revolution truly is, we will come to understand the gravity of our actions, our micro revolutions, and know that our value exists and our efforts are needed. It is through such recognition that we will contribute to changing our social existence and creating a more just world.

# CHAPTER 3

## *The Making of a Revolutionary*
### Amy Hoyt

My mother claims that I was born a revolutionary. Her favorite anecdote to tell about me is one of my earliest memories and involves a most unfortunate miscalculation on my part regarding natural consequences. As a toddler, I was quite unhappy when, as she lovingly rocked and nursed my younger sister, she sent me to take a nap. I may have taken off my messy diaper and smeared the contents all over my room. I still gag when changing dirty diapers as a result of the two-hour self-directed cleaning fiasco that ensued. I don't know whether I agree that I was born a revolutionary, but I believe that several distinct events in my life propelled me toward insurgency.

As a young girl, I was sexually assaulted by an older boy who came to live with our family as part of the "Indian Placement Program."[1] He arrived in autumn each year and silently terrorized me in our home until the end of spring, when he would return to spend the summer with his family of origin. I believed him when he said that he would kill me if I told anyone. I kept that secret until I was grown and safely out of the house. As a juvenile insurgent in training, I

---

[1] The Indian Placement Program was a cross-cultural foster-care program administered by the Mormon Church that placed Native American children in white Mormon homes. Studies conducted of the program reveal both its positive and negative effects on those involved.

learned critical skills such as secrecy and problem solving. I learned
to self-medicate with alcohol in order to exist in a violent, sexually
abusive environment. Living in a devout Latter-day Saints (LDS)
home without access to alcohol posed some challenges, but I have
never been afraid of hard work, as my parents still remind me. I was
creative and managed to get my "prescriptions" filled. I had to learn
the art of deception and the ability to navigate many precarious situations, which proved to be another ripe training ground for a future
revolutionary. I also honed the ability to truly commit to something:
I was an excellent alcoholic.

Eventually, after years of substance abuse, an observant LDS
church leader asked if he could speak to me. He asked me about my
life and promised that as an ecclesiastical leader he would hold my
secrets safe. We began to meet once a week. He told me about his
grown daughter and her struggle with addiction as well as her
eventual recovery. In time, he convinced me to invite my parents to
our meetings. I reluctantly agreed that it was probably time to get
help. I wasn't ready to reveal all of the ugliness, but I was ready to get
sober. My parents lovingly cared for me and helped me stop drinking.
In time, I was able to tell them about the sexual abuse, something
that, understandably, spiritually unmoored my mother for several
years. Sobriety helped me renew my relationship with God. My higher
power was critical to my well-being and it seemed that my religion of
origin, Mormonism, was a good fit for my newfound spiritual awak-
ening.

A few years later, feeling stronger and more self-assured. I began
dating. Despite my wayward youth, I had managed to internalize the
pervasive messages aimed at LDS teens about the importance of marriage and creating heterosexual families. Marriage was of God, marriage was good, and marriage in an LDS temple was particularly
blessed. Preparation for this eventuality was the righteous goal of all
Latter-day Saints.

I dutifully married a man I met at church. We married in an LDS
temple. I took his name, washed his clothes, supported his dreams,
and lost weight in an attempt to gain his elusive approval. He had sex

with other people, pretended he had cancer, and beat me and told me it was my fault. My culpability was a familiar idea since I had spent years blaming myself for sexual abuse. Despite the hard work I had done in recovery, somehow I regressed and believed that I had inadvertently "asked" for abuse—sexual, physical, and emotional. After two years, many bruises, and an episode that left me unconscious from strangulation, my mother packed my bags and moved me out. I was hesitant to leave; divorce in the LDS Church is serious, and a temple "cancellation" meant obtaining permission from the highest church authorities. My reluctance was mitigated by my knowledge that my husband and I would get back together eventually. I knew we would work it out. We had been married in an LDS temple and our vows were considered to last beyond death, which incidentally was inching closer for me with each violent argument. But he was so very sorry for hitting, choking, cheating, and lying. He was never going to hurt me again. This was good news since we were committed for eternity.

While I waited for my husband to get sober and recover from his fake cancer, I decided to attend college. I headed off to Brigham Young University (BYU) to get an education. I wanted to be in a religious environment while I planned my inevitable marital reunion. College was a bit different than I expected. I was a married woman without a spouse at a university divided into singletons and married couples. Housing, activities, and congregations are all determined by one's gender and/or marital status. I didn't fit into either category, as I was "separated" from my eternal companion. It was a difficult and lonely time, particularly since my mother was battling cancer at the time (real, actual cancer). I worked hard to navigate learning, forgiving, and making friends.

I can still conjure up the sense of exhilaration I had upon being exposed to my first piece of feminist analysis. My older sister, who was also at BYU, gave me an article she was assigned in her women's studies class. It took my breath away. I needed to know more. I needed to understand this language of human dignity and worth; this rhetoric of equality and parity. I marched in my first Take Back the Night rally two months later. I filed for divorce and began to resurrect my inner revolutionary.

Soon after my conversion to feminism, I transferred to the University of Utah, where I enrolled as a women's studies major. I cried through my first class. It felt like I had finally found a treasure I had been searching for my entire life. To no avail, I had looked for it at home, at church, in therapy, and in twelve-step meetings. While I had found beautiful and important gems in these locales, this was the mother lode of all booty! I had found my social, political, genealogical roots. I was liberated by an academic community rooted in elevating the status of women, and simultaneously overcome by sorrow for the price I had paid.

Then the anger came. In hindsight, this was inevitable. Having much more experience with grief over the past twenty years, I might have warned my younger self that anger was to be expected. I couldn't attend church at this time. I couldn't stomach sitting in church and listening to men dominate discussions with their opinions, inevitably couched in the guise of theological certainty. Every false tradition, misogynist opinion, and human flaw of men in my congregation seemed magnified in my eyes. I was so tired of male privilege. I didn't go back for two years. My personal relationship with my higher power became primary during this time. I read scriptures and prayed every day. I wanted God in my life, unfiltered through institutional and congregational prejudice. My time in twelve-step meetings helped me recognize that defining God was essential to my spiritual health. And in defining God, I looked toward the Latter-day Saint belief in a Mother in Heaven; a female partner to the male God, equal in glory and value. God, in my view, was both male and female. I was *their* daughter. Our relationship was familial, not patriarchal.

Still disillusioned with organized religion, I graduated from the University of Utah and moved to Minnesota to do a master's degree in women's studies. I loved my program. I was surrounded by a cohort of intelligent, independent students and professors. I learned to speak up in class and to voice agreement and dissent by using theoretical and experiential evidence. It was empowering and exciting. My passion for the field grew along with my confidence in the power of my voice.

During this time, I questioned my ability to partner again in a heterosexual marriage. I confided in my orthodox parents that I wasn't sure if I could personally (re)embrace the theology of the traditional Mormon family. To my pleasant surprise, they simply listened and told me how much they loved me. My uncertainty about my own ability to participate in heterosexual love was, of course, based upon my past. I desperately wanted to avoid repeating any prior experiences I had with my first husband. I now realize that this was naïve. The time I have spent in subsequent years with my two queer brothers and many queer friends has shown me that all relationships have the potential for power differential, deception, and infidelity. Unfortunately, I have come to understand that humans possess an infinite ability to hurt one another, regardless of sexual orientation, race, ethnicity, religion, and gender.

My mother came to visit me while I was in graduate school and invited me to attend church with her. I reluctantly agreed, mostly because I knew it was important to her and because she was my guest. As I sat in the familiar pews and listened to the opening hymn, I wept. Stunned by my tears, I realized that while I had maintained a relationship with God, I had desperately missed the sense of community that can be cultivated within a congregation. Perhaps I had underestimated the gems I had found in a religious community? When viewed in concert, these singular stones formed an invaluable treasure. I knew that this treasure was as valuable and important to me as the treasure I had found within feminism.

My revolutionary self got to work. Within feminist theoretical circles, I was the insurgent questioning why religion couldn't be integrated into feminist theory. In Mormon circles, I questioned why women were given such narrow roles. These seemingly different locales I inhabited allowed me to find new iterations of my voice. I argued with my feminist theory professor that radical theologian Mary Daly was misguided in calling for separation from men: we need to work together in order to overcome the dysfunction of the rule of the fathers. I argued with my LDS friends that women's roles needed to be expanded and that their voices needed to be integrated into all aspects of the church. It was an exciting time, yet a bit disorienting to inhabit this in-between space. As I prepared to apply for PhD programs, I knew one thing—I did not want to study Mormonism as a career. I wasn't ready to make this hybrid existence part of my permanent future.

Despite my reservations, I found myself in a new PhD program that combined women's studies and religion. I moved to California and began the arduous process of becoming vetted by the academy to be brought into the scholarly fold. I loved my courses, my advisor, and my colleagues. It was a remarkable experience that encouraged greater integration of my feminist and religious identities. Supported by my female classmates, I dipped my toe into the fraught history of Mormon feminism. It was unsettling to learn of the excommunications of Mormon feminist scholars and to grapple with the possibility that this could be my future. Revolutionaries in Mormonism do not fare well. I worked hard to figure out how I could engage feminism and remain faithful to a tradition that I loved and valued.

I continued to attend church and deepen my personal relationship with God and a community of believers. The anger was starting to dissipate and was being replaced by quiet reflection. I learned to look for pieces of God and Christ that I could hold on to and to discard rhetoric that unwittingly propped up the hierarchical, gendered divisions of an organized religion. I began to look for commonality among fellow parishioners and forge friendships based, in part, on a mutual devotion to our faith tradition. When someone's comments really bothered me or I knew they were theologically inaccurate, I would make note to talk to the person privately or would respectfully offer an alternate reading of the same theological principle. I was learning where I fit within Mormonism and how I could make both feminism and religion work to enrich my life.

During this time, I met a remarkable person, someone whose sense of calm and kindness helped me to continue to heal and find nuanced ways of thinking about men. Eventually, we married in a small ceremony, surrounded by our families. I did not take his name, nor did I wash his clothes or lose weight. But I gave him my whole self: a thoughtful, independent, feminist, Mormon woman. And he loved me just as I was. His love was without condition and his acceptance of me was boundless. Nothing scared him, and his adoration for me was apparent. I knew that God had prepared him for me, and I for him.

I continued my studies and graduated with a PhD in women's studies in religion. I had my first child during graduate school and participated in graduation ceremonies four years later, clothed in the robes of maternity and educational accomplishment. Over the next several years, we had more children and I learned a new type of community: family. I vowed to make our family a safe place—free from abuse and condemnation; a place where boys and girls are valued equally and are given the opportunity to flourish spiritually, intellectually, and emotionally. This community is where I distill all of my theory, experience, and practice. Activism starts here. Revolution begins with these people as I learn to forge new ways of being Mormon and feminist.

I was not born a revolutionary. I was refined and honed through the tumult of abuse and the iniquities of men. My insurgency allowed for hope and a closer relationship with God. The cost was not cheap. Out of the misery of sexual, physical, and emotional abuse, I grew empathetic, compassionate, and committed to justice. I also eventually learned to love myself. My communities of faith, feminism, and family have helped me craft a worldview that seeks to honor God by privileging those commands that point us toward human dignity, worth, community, and seeking out the "other."

As I view my life from a distance, I see a complex and muddled map peppered with danger, distractions, and merciless pirates. But what I chose to pay attention to—what is most evident to me—are the priceless treasures that continue to sustain me as I struggle against those who use power as a weapon and perpetuate gender-based violence in all its forms.

CHAPTER 4

# The Alchemy of Survival
### Edyka Chilomé

Over hundreds of years, the religion known as Christianity has become a powerhouse that influences the very core of what many of us consider reality in the Americas. It is commonly understood that believing in a God informs the ethical and moral culture of individuals who make up a larger society. Some have believed and continue to believe that stealing land and killing those who refuse to agree with them—the doctrine of Manifest Destiny, the occupation of Palestine, and the Spanish Crusades come to mind—is their divine right for the good of humanity. When they are armed with the word of God in one hand and a gun in the other, who dares stop them?

More than five hundred years after a violent Christian inquisition and war on indigenous peoples in the Americas, I was born into the United Methodist Church, a large, wealthy, predominantly white institution with an extensive history of savage racism, particularly in the US South. My indigenous mestiza mother found her way into this place as a reactionary measure of survival. I imagine her calling to be a pastor came in the same breath as her desire to know more than the large agricultural slave fields of the southwest. Her choice to assimilate into a wealthy white institution mirrored the actions of many indigenous and/or African women before her who would run willingly into the violent Christian church to survive and escape the induced poverty, genocide, and condemnation that surrounded them.

In my essay, "What Has Remained: A Testimony of a Mujer Mestiza," I speak passionately of how my mothers and ancestors, against all odds, managed to use the institutional church not only to survive as colonized people but also as a spiritual technology to creatively pass down indigenous principles of solidarity and survival.[1] I speak honestly of the ways my elders managed to model political resistance through spiritual activism and liberation theology within the Christian church. Their example and work called me to walk with our pueblo and continue the struggle of our ancestors. I proudly and gratefully claim this inheritance as a major influence in my work as an artivist (artist as activist). Yet in this essay, I do not speak of the cost of this resistance and refuge, nor do I speak of the inheritance of loss that accompanies the privilege of surviving this kind of war.

The war against indigenous peoples in the Americas—instigated and justified by the Christian church and related capitalist imperial enterprises—has been taking place for more than five hundred years. Yet we are not given the social or historical reference points to acknowledge the side effects of a systemic war that has been and continues to be carried out through generations like a domino effect. This war has played and continues to play out through horrific rates of murder, rape, displacement, human trafficking, incarceration, land theft, land degradation, cultural/spiritual erasure, and psychological violence against Natives. We live its side effects every day with mass depression, suicidal thoughts, addiction, insecurity, alienation, fragmented families and communities, deteriorating physical health, psychological imbalances, and abusive and violent behavior. None of us is absolved from this reality as colonized and displaced people—not the elders, not my mother, not the activist pastor of whom I speak so lovingly in the context of resistance and political action, and certainly not myself.

---

[1] Erica Granados De La Rosa, "What Has Remained: The Testimony of a Mujer Mestiza"," in *Faithfully Feminist: Jewish, Christian, and Muslim Feminists on Why We Stay*, ed. Gina Messina-Dysert, Jennifer Zobair, and Amy Levine, Vol. 1, *I Speak For Myself Inc.* (Ashland, OR: White Cloud, 2015), 102–8.

I often speak candidly about my first suicide attempt at age eight. I have a memory of asking my older brother what chemical under the sink would kill me if ingested. I was a highly empathic child living in an extremely unstable and neglectful home based in the disorienting culture of the United States. Since my earliest memories, my mother and I suffered from grave depression, and the relationship between her and my father was a source of constant turmoil and pain, even after their divorce early in my life. My mother's constant emotional and physical absence in the life of her children suggested a complex relationship with her role as mother—something I suspect she had little agency in choosing for herself.

My father was a refugee of the civil war in El Salvador and my mother the child of poor migrant field workers who earned slave wages. They were both raised in abusive homes where emotional, physical, and sexual abuses were commonplace. They also were constantly displaced as children, my father given away for some years and forced out of his country due to US-funded warfare, my mother also constantly displaced by induced poverty caused by US capital interests. The amount of violence they had already encountered before my older brother and I were born is overwhelming to consider. Yet they surpassed the expectations placed on them and worked hard to climb up a glorified socioeconomic ladder that promised to lead them and their children to some type of freedom and humanity.

Although at some point in their lives my parents were politically active around issues like immigration reform and transnational solidarity work inside and outside of the church, there were still explosive silences that crippled and damaged all of us to the point of no return. And at some point, no one did return. After years of processing a nasty and violent divorce, which to my knowledge included kidnaping, child abandonment, and neglect, I was left alone at sixteen with no consistent relationship or contact with any member of my family and little understanding of what the hell had happened. I spent many years attempting to understand the factors that broke up my politically inclined family and left me to fend for myself at such a tender age. Often, I feel it might be easier to digest had my family been explicitly targeted by direct political opposition. Although I admittedly cannot say with certainty that this was not the case, I am left to believe that the situation of my family was much more insidious, much more covert and internalized than what we can often comprehend.

It was not until my early twenties, while I was working as a case manager at a domestic violence shelter, that I was able to witness the ways generational trauma works to fragment us and keep us emotionally stunted in our lives, regardless of the socioeconomic class we are able to achieve or what "radical" political movement we are a part of. Working at a shelter made me privy to the intimate details of diverse women who struggled with addiction and self-inflicted abuse, often due to being abused themselves or witnessing the behavior of a mother or caretaker who was abused.

I was often told by older employees that it was not uncommon to witness mother, daughter, and granddaughter come through the shelter at different points with similar or amplified psychological, emotional, and physical health issues. Now imagine this cycle repeated for generations over five hundred years. Imagine these cycles of internalized and external violence playing out in the lives of colonized people who witnessed mass genocide and slavery, and who through generations continue to witness the vestiges of an abusive system obsessed with power and control.

In my own family, I witnessed the ways abuse cycled in the behavior of my parents and in myself. I learned how distrust and fear eroded the possibilities of love and connection. I learned how we can become addicted to shame and loneliness, elements that cripple the imaginative possibilities of change. I learned that I began to live what psychology calls the wounded healers syndrome. I was relentlessly dedicated to healing everyone and everything but myself. Yet the worlds I traveled would not let me forget how much I hurt and how much I was expected to fight just to exist.

As I began to seek more information on my identity and history as a woman of color in the movement for change, I learned that the cycles of historical violence, particularly for colonized and racialized women, have been unforgiving and chronic. We find ourselves constantly in spaces of violence, whether in dominant institutions, political movements, faith communities, or our own homes and bedrooms. We have little turnover time to internally deal with immediate trauma and little to no resource to vocalize or heal the wounds that we inherited from our mothers and our families. Moreover, as a displaced people, the wealth found in rooted community and relationships with our families and our land is taken from us as we are forced to reinvent ourselves as "foreigners" in strange new worlds where we are often not welcomed.

Having been given the tools to name realities of oppression and violence through my parents' activism, it became necessary for me to contextualize the violent fragmentation of my life within a larger historical context. It became important for me to take the time and understand, even if only superficially, the trauma that lives in my mother-line and in my family as a whole. Taking the time to recollect and acknowledge out loud helped me find compassion and forgiveness, basic tools to counsel the rage in myself. This recollecting provided some answers and comfort in my desperate search for home and healing that I could not seem to find no matter how many protests I organized or attended.

Like my parents, I slowly began to choose for myself how to embody the act of resistance and survival independent of cultural expectations. I, too, began to search for freedom amid the shattered pieces of my constantly changing reality. Coming from a family with stories too painful to tell, I have come to define freedom in the careful study of self, in the weaving of broken memories and spoken prayers. I have come to know freedom in the fragmented shards of mirror I have been courageous enough to collect along the way. I have learned that I, like my mother, have been molded by the compassionate rhythms of change, thrust into the painful impossibilities of this life, and carefully crafted into miracle. We are creatures of faith simply because we know our life to be miraculous in a world where we are constantly reminded we should not exist. I have found power in a faith that affirms the whole of me with my complexity and my brokenness. I have painfully come to know the beauty in naming myself even as I change form like my ancestors, even as I become water in the midst of a drowning world, even if, against all odds, I survive bruised and broken.

In this life, I have worked and continue working to heal the fragmentations of my past and my present. This is no easy task, yet I prioritize my mental, physical, emotional, and spiritual health as an offering to my ancestors and as a gift to my descendants. I believe, as our people have always believed, that the change I embody in this generation will heal and strengthen the generations behind us and in front of us. This is how I have chosen to live out my faith and my political consciousness. I have found that our resistance lies in our existence, yet our revolution lies in walking full circle into whole, into center, into healing the war-torn worlds inside of us that lie scattered through generations.

We must honor the worlds we have walked and touched and changed, and that have walked and touched and changed us. Our constant form has always been change in all its fragmented complexities. We have come to know this without being able to read or write. We have known this before Columbus came, and even when the African kings came before Columbus. In the beginning of our consciousness, we looked up at the stars and knew nothing remained the same and everything was in movement. So, too, our great creating spirit, our God, is change. It is through this change that we have learned the alchemy of survival.

CHAPTER 5

# The Matter of Power:
## Organizing as Women of Faith of Color
### Mollie Costello and Sandhya Jha

*Note: This essay is written in interview style with each author reporting on the other as well as points where their work is jointly narrated. Subheadings alert the reader to changes in voice. Enjoy!*

The city of Oakland, California, is the activist's wildest fantasy, and the city of Oakland will break an activist's heart over and over. Oakland's powerful organizing history includes:

- Liberty Hall in Oakland is the last remaining building in the country to have housed a chapter of the Marcus Garvey–led United Negro Improvement Association (UNIA);
- C. L. Dellums, one of the earliest leaders of the Brotherhood of Sleeping Car Porters, was from Oakland; and
- the Black Panther Party was founded by Oaklanders Huey Newton and Bobby Seale.

But in a city that increasingly resents civil rights activists as disrupting "revitalization," we don't always remember why the UNIA exists. In the late 1800s, many black leaders did not think the United States could ever confront its own racism effectively enough to make a safe home for blacks. We sometimes also forget that Dellums was fired from his job as a sleeping car porter in 1929 because he got involved with a union. A union that had the audacity to demand things like customers referring to black porters by their real names instead of calling them all "George." And while we debate the armed nature of the Panthers, we rarely discuss the fact that they came into existence because in Oakland in the 1960s, white officers would not patrol black neighborhoods except to harass, intimidate, and shake down young black men, while refusing to respond to calls for help from those same communities.

In fact, the story goes, when Henry Kaiser sought to build ship-yards in Oakland and Richmond, California, during WWII, he sought the most productive laborers to work at those plants: he went to the South and recruited black sharecroppers who knew hard work. Recognizing that he was about to transform the demographics of those cities, while he was visiting the South, he recruited a police force who would know how to manage sharecroppers in their new home. He recruited Jim Crow–trained police to move to Oakland and Richmond and join the force. Now, a lot of the activists in Oakland working to create racial equity and justice are nonreligious, but the fact of the matter is that to be an organizer in Oakland means having a great deal of faith in the face of this history, a history that continues to play itself out today.

As organizers and ministers, we have faith, despite ourselves. There is certainly a church community that buoys that faith, but where we practice our faith is in the neighborhood. In fact, the main reason we are in a church is because we first encountered that church in the neighborhood. The two of us may have met at an action for the Justice for Alan Blueford Coalition, or we may have met at First Con-gregational Church of Oakland when Sandhya was preaching. Oak-land is a city of 400,000, but it's also a small town for the activist set and a small town for the spiritual progressive set. The Venn diagram of the two groups meant that the two of us were destined to be friends and comrades.

## Meet Mollie

Mollie is founder and director of the Alan Blueford Center for Justice. The Bible story that might describe Mollie best is the parable of the persistent widow (Luke 18:1–8), where the woman shows up before a judge who neither fears God nor has compassion, and she keeps showing up until the judge finally relents and gives her the justice she seeks just so she'll leave him alone. Mollie knew and sat with the family of Alan Blueford in the days and weeks and months after Alan, an eighteen-year-old just about to graduate from Skyline High School, was shot and killed by a police officer who then shot himself in the foot, pretending he killed Alan in self-defense. Mollie spoke up alongside Alan's family and other coalition members at city council meeting after city council meeting, demanding justice apply to the corrupt officer, compensation for the family, and an overhaul of a police system so corrupt and mismanaged that the federal government put it into receivership (that is, the federal government took custody of the department because the city could no longer be trusted to manage it). Mollie's persistence did not end there: she began a community center to remember Alan and to foster strong young leaders in the community who will not just demand but create justice in our community.

## Meet Sandhya

Sandhya pastored First Christian Church of Oakland (not First Congregational, where Sandhya and Mollie know each other from, described in the next section) for seven years. She started out with the dream of taking the ten people left in that 40,000-square-foot facility and helping them catch a spirit of renewal and desire to participate in God's radical work of liberation. She hoped to take the beleaguered and scared people in the upper room and nudge them into being Pentecost people, connecting to people of every culture and sharing with them the possibility of a community driven by God's abundant and all-inclusive love. When it became clear the congregation was not passionate about changing significantly in order to be the church that the community needed, she asked a different question. What did the church want its legacy to be?

The remaining members had grown up in Oakland and lived through the ongoing violence: they wanted to create peace in the midst of violence. Knowing that God is at work in the community, Sandhya helped the congregation turn their building into a collective of forty different nonprofits all working to create access, opportunity, and dignity as the means of creating peace in the Bay Area. Sandhya wanted her ministry to be helping a Saul congregation become a Paul congregation; instead, her ministry ended up primarily helping her church avoid being the rich young ruler that clung to his possessions in ways that limited the building up of the Kingdom of God.

## Meeting and Finding Common Cause

First Congregational Church of Oakland, or First Congo, as the church is fondly referred to, came onto Mollie's radar because one of its active leaders, Nichola Torbett, showed up for the Justice for Alan Blueford Coalition in real, risking-arrest ways. And Sandhya preaches there regularly. Mollie found herself thinking maybe this was a church where people walked the walk, where Mollie might get to be her full self—her full spiritual and activist and feminist and embodied self. Because that's not guaranteed in churches.

The Justice for Alan Blueford Coalition did not come from his home church. Alan Blueford's family faithfully participated in a large church in East Oakland for years. Alan's preschool was a foregone conclusion: he attended the preschool at the church. But when Alan's life came to a brutal end a week before he was supposed to graduate from high school, his pastor and his church didn't show up for him or his family, didn't demand justice and full accounting from the city, even though the pastor had power and influence among elected officials. Standing up for Alan would have cost the pastor regular access to the police chief and potentially city and state funding for social service projects. Standing up for Alan would have cost the pastor and church power they had worked so hard to capture for the sake of senior housing and youth programming and the preschool Alan had attended. Standing up for Alan would have cost them power that their pastor courted by briefly campaigning for a Republican governor.

And there it is: power. The thing that makes decisions for us. The thing that justifies the decisions we make. The thing that creates a sense of foregone conclusions. The thing we think we're all defining the same way—even those of us in the church—which God defines in a completely different way.

There is nothing glamorous about having no power. Many of the people we work with day to day have been told they have no power, and so have we. Many of the people we work with have been told they don't deserve power, and so have we. Our community includes children in foster care whose fates are decided by harried strangers. It includes young black and Latino boys whose slightest misbehaviors have gotten them expelled from kindergarten. It includes LGBTQ youth who have been kicked out of their faithful Christian homes and into the streets. It includes girls who have been told throughout their lives that they are unworthy of love until they run away and meet a pimp (sometimes not much older than them) who tells them he loves them and then lets them know that if they love him, they'll help him earn some money by standing on International Boulevard until someone buys them for an hour or so. It includes black and brown men and women who have experienced police harassment and brutality and have lost family members to police-related murders as well as street violence and domestic violence. It includes Asian, Latino, and African immigrants and refugees who contribute immensely to our infrastructure and live in constant fear of whether they can stay together with their own families for yet another day. It includes returned citizens, formerly incarcerated people, who are not allowed to live with family members if their family members live in federally funded homes and who are not allowed interviews for most jobs in the community.

Our community includes many hurt people who hurt people, people seeking dignity and people seeking control, people seeking to build themselves up and seeking to tear each other down. A sense of powerlessness and a desire for power sometimes drive these actions at the same time that most of the decisions are made by people with power who never question why they have it or whether they should have it. Many of those decisions are made to preserve power for some people at the expense of others. For example, police officers' associations do not create space for restorative justice in communities, functionally requiring officers to uniformly support any police-related violence for the sake of preserving bargaining power, keeping dangerous officers in the system, and punishing officers who speak out against unaccountable behavior on the force.

Both of us have been part of systems that sought to take away or negate our power (Mollie as a nurse at a major hospital and Sandhya as a pastor); both of us have navigated the complex intersection of privilege and marginality of being light-skinned mixed-race women of color. Both of us seek to strengthen in others the same thing we strengthen in ourselves: an awareness of personal power and an ability to honor the power of others so that together we can transform our communities.

Here's where our faith matters the most in the work we're doing: we have the gift of knowing that God defines power differently than men do. (God probably defines power differently than most women do, too, but definitely differently than men.) And we have seen God's definition of power tangibly in the work we do, when we do it from a place of authenticity and a place of love.

## Redefining Power
### Sandhya's Story

Sandhya works with a multifaith organization to create policies that preserve the dignity of immigrants in our community. The immigrants she works with either fled dangerous situations or could not find a way to support their families in their country of origin on a continent shaped by US policies that limit other nations' economic possibilities for US gain. They contribute to this economy while supporting families in their motherland, whether they are here legally or not. US residents rely on immigrants' low-wage work for cheap goods and services while demonizing them in political discourse. Our economy is built on their labor, and some of them have read enough of the Bible to know that God values them fully as God's beloved children. Therefore, our political systems should as well. And so they organize and advocate, and the faith community organizes and advocates alongside them.

Our county's sheriff is hostile to immigrants and for years participated in something called "ICE holds": if someone was pulled over for something like a faulty taillight or speeding, and if Immigration and Customs Enforcement (ICE) had that person on a list of undocumented immigrants, the sheriff had them jailed overnight, long enough for ICE to show up and put them into detention. No matter how many letters the faith community sent, no matter how many community events the organization held, the sheriff refused to meet with them. Showing up at his office yet again, fatigued and desperate, the group—including people who were undocumented immigrants themselves—sat down in the grass outside his office. They prayed silently and fervently that he would finally listen to them. It may be that the sheriff saw them outside his window and felt embarrassed, or it may be that as a Catholic, he recognized people praying and identified with them. It may be that the Holy Spirit blew through his office. But in that moment two years ago he met with them and heard their stories and prayers, and he ultimately reversed his position.

## Mollie's Story

On the day after Thanksgiving 2014, Mollie was part of a group called the Black Friday 14. They took over a Bay Area Rapid Transit (BART) station and shut down trains for almost four hours (in honor of the four hours that young Michael Brown lay dead in the street after his murder by police officers in Ferguson, Missouri, in August that year). This was on the biggest shopping day of the year, a day people from the rest of the Bay Area flood into San Francisco to enjoy decorations and cash in on great holiday shopping deals. As the fourteen black community leaders were arrested and taken (ironically, on a BART train) to the nearest police station to be processed through the system, they shared with the police officers their rationale for taking this stance. They looked the officers in the eyes and shared stories of people lost to police violence. And they witnessed the tears in the eyes of the officers who recognized the humanity of the victims and their families, some of them being parents themselves.

## God's Definition of Power

We live in a community saturated with a very particular way of determining power: power over others, power to get what we need even if that means keeping those things from others, power to get as much as we can for as little cost as possible (financially, physically, or emotionally). We live in a community where there are winners and losers. And today more than ever in its history, our city is steeped in people with power moving into the city, not recognizing their power, and not recognizing how their power and agency are pushing out whole communities of people with less money and therefore less power.

We're saddened by the schisms that show up within the movement for justice. We've joked that the right wing doesn't need to divide us; we do it ourselves. We divide ourselves particularly through *purity politics* (Sandhya's term): people needing for everyone else to use the same language they use and the same tactics, or else those other people aren't considered *really* part of the movement. We watch divisions within the groups we work with, whether it be Black Lives Matter or housing justice organizations. Even the most radical among us are vulnerable to the politics of power: how it gets wielded, who is allowed to wield it, and what bright lines divide us even when we are on the same side of an issue.

But we're fueling the revolution with a different sort of power. It is the power of self-love and other-love. It is the power of demanding accountability but not relying on those with power to give it up, because our power comes from within and from each other. It is the power of a God who can move the hearts even of our adversaries if we speak and act always authentically, boldly, and out of love (even if that love includes righteous outrage at injustice). It is the power of our sister wading into the Pacific Ocean and dedicating her life to Christ and her community and the constant fight for her own liberation and all of ours.

On September 1, 2015, the two of us watched the sun set on the beach in Alameda, California, as we participated in the baptism of a beloved sister of ours. She had written her own baptismal vows, including the following: "Will you strive for justice, peace, and freedom among all people, accepting the freedom and power God gives to resist evil, injustice, and oppression?" We prayed to the four directions, we called in the ancestors, we invited elders to bless our sister, and she sang "I give my life away" before walking into the Pacific Ocean to be baptized into a life in Christ and into a life of self—and other—liberation. What's true for both of us is that there is nowhere we would have rather been that day . . . and that we know there are very few spaces like that particular church that could create just that kind of baptism.

Che Guevara is quoted as saying, "at the risk of sounding ridiculous, the true revolutionary is guided by great feelings of love." We're set up not to love each other. And perhaps the most revolutionary act we create isn't in the streets or in the faces of police or elected officials. Perhaps it is in the subtle ways that we reject the "us versus them" paradigm the world tries to force on us, knowing that it is a false construct. It is the way we (sometimes gingerly) create connections between radicals and moderates in our programs and events and in our physical spaces. (Even harder can be creating connections between radicals, the way Mollie did when three different socialist groups sought to support the Justice for Alan Blueford Coalition but fought among themselves. Mollie had to remind them that no one but them saw their differences and that they were there because of what they actually agreed upon.)

We spend so much time fighting against ourselves on the edges of this movement, when love is our strongest weapon for ending the systems we seek to resist. And that is what people with power have been trying to kill since the days of the plantation, by tearing apart families generation after generation. It is what people with power have done by pitting each generation of immigrants against black Americans so that we do not realize how our experiences and our future are enmeshed. And so we choose to create love, unity, and community as the foundation of all of our justice work. What we're best known for is our protesting. Our most important work, though, might be the work of weaving people together, not getting trapped in purity politics, and trying in our own way to undo the trap that is purity politics.

We create spaces for young people to be creative as well as fight oppression. We create spaces for people to really get to know each other on a deep level, to trust each other as well as stand up for their rights. We are facing down the economic violence and state-sanctioned violence that result in intracommunity violence in our streets; we are facing down capitalism's contempt for our humanity. And Audre Lorde's statement remains true today that "the master's tools will never dismantle the master's house."[1] So we need to use different tools and build a very different foundation. Those tools might take us in some scary directions if we stay true to them. (What does it mean to contemplate the possibility of a restorative justice process where genuinely repentant police and the families of their victims could begin to create healing together?) But we know that using the master's version of power will ultimately harm those on the margins more than those with that kind of power.

THE monumental, defining, all-important, essential *revolutionary act* we have to do as humans is to use our immense collective cognitive powers to find a way to *stop burning each other with the fire*

---

[1] She goes on to point out that even if we beat him at his own game temporarily, we're still playing his game. Audre Lorde, "The Master's Tools Will Never Dismantle the Master's House"," *Sister Outsider: Essays and Speeches* (1984; repr., Berkeley, CA: Crossing, 2007), 110–14

*(the power) we discovered how to harness over 100,000 years ago.* After we discovered how to control fire as early humans, we continued to advance, in terms of the power we can leverage (wind, solar, nuclear) and the places we can venture (to the ocean depths and to the moon and beyond). Where have those billions of dollar and millennia of intellectual wrestling landed us? They've landed us where we are now: a time of once-again growing inequity and codified injustice. In the name of God, because God is Love, it is time to harness the energies of Love.

The two of us harbor a mixture of pride and sadness that the modern-day civil rights movement, the Black Lives Matter movement, is led primarily by women of color (and specifically queer and immigrant-connected black women). We are proud because it is a powerful women-led movement. While US white nationalist history often tells the story of abolition and civil rights as a male-only movement, there were many women who led as well, such as Harriet Tubman, Sojourner Truth, Ida B. Wells, Fannie Lou Hamer, Ella Baker, Rosa Parks, Dorothy Height, Coretta Scott King, Ericka Huggins, and many others. Part of the reason for the visibility of women's leadership, and that of trans and queer folk, in Black Lives Matter can be attributed to legal, political, and cultural changes in women's access to power. In our opinion, it is also affected by the New Jim Crow, which has placed so many black and brown men behind bars.[2] There is something deeply horizontal, though, about the modern-day civil rights movement, something deeply relational that indicates that different understanding of power in a women-led movement. It is about "low ego, high impact" and being a leader-full movement. It is about black self-love and black other-love and about solidarity from Asian and Latino and even Anglo allies without misappropriation of leadership. There are men as well as women embracing these values, but there is

---

[2] The *New Jim Crow* is a term coined by Michelle Alexander in her book, *The New Jim Crow: Mass Incarceration in the Age of Colorblindness* (New York: New Press, 2010). It is our opinion that it took brutal systemic racism locking up a generation of black and brown men before the leadership of black and brown women could shine through the patriarchy that muted their voices for generations in the fight for racial justice.

something about women's power that shapes a movement differently, we suspect.

It is the same kind of power we have found—not in very many churches but in a special one, a church that gives both of us compassion when we are fatigued, gentle embrace when we feel battered, and that pushes us out the door to do God's justice, but does not push us out there alone. It is the power of God for the sake of God's people. We hope to encounter it in church, but we do encounter it in the streets every day.

# CHAPTER 6

## *The Smallness of Radicalism*
### Kate McElwee

For three years, a group of African theologians gathered as a research project to develop, model, and sustain a new methodology and process for theological reflection, research, and study at the service of the African Church and the global Roman Catholic Church. On the occasion of the third year, I was invited as an observer to the colloquium, which took place at Hakima College in Nairobi, Kenya. Thirty-six theologians gathered in the spirit of a family reunion, reporting on the fruits of their work inspired by the energies shared the previous year.

I have been in many Catholic spaces where a magnetism of scarcity draws the women together, but in this very equitable group, I was surprised by an announcement inviting the women of the colloquium to meet independently for a small caucus. We shared a meal together, while the men cheekily tried to join, and then gathered in the corner of the room to discuss how to stay connected and how to help each other. An email list was circulated and in minutes, a women's caucus was formed. I am pretty sure that is the revolution in motion: women and nonbinary people claiming space and identity as Catholics. Setting the intention to help each other.

In our women's huddle, Ghanaian feminist theologian Mercy Amba Oduyoye offered the sage advice that we should continue to meet as women in theology, to mentor one another, to publish, and promote one another. There was a strong emphasis on getting our writings as women theologians into print, and furthermore, helping to get published those women who are perhaps not as connected as those of us who gathered at the colloquium. This ethos was described as "a willingness to feed oneself and to feed others."

For women theologians, the emphasis on writing and publishing speaks both to the importance of narrative theology and to the power of language. Part of the revolution for greater gender equity in religion comes from refusing to let sacred words and stories be defined to exclude women: weaving the resources and experiences that the Catholic Church rejects or androcentrifies into a theology that resonates. Claiming words like *priest, disciple, Catholic,* and even *woman* means we are writing the narrative of experience and theology for ourselves.

In all, we met for about ten minutes and then went back to the paper presentations and dialogue of the meetings. As we made our way back to the main meeting space, a sister from Kenya in the final year of her doctorate program grabbed my arm and whispered, "the Catholic Church is the most oppressive institution against women in the world! Do you think I want to wear this? My bishop makes me wear this, while he wears whatever he wants." Habited in a local or domestic order, this sister will join the ranks of a small group of religious women in Africa to receive her doctorate in theology. I will always remember this unprompted disclosure, especially when uninformed Western feminists try to explain why Africans are not part of their movement by claiming "Africa is not ready."

What surprised me most about the sister's disclosure was that she did not know about either my work with the Women's Ordination Conference (WOC) or my feminism. As an observer at this meeting, I listened during the presentations and spoke carefully and minimally about my work during break times. As an organizer, I felt it was most important to note the language and words theologians used about women in the Church, especially in the art of speaking about ordination without saying "ordination." In U.S. English-speaking contexts, ordination is subtly couched or hidden in "governance," "sacramental equality," and "leadership." There is a common fear that talking about "women's issues" will lead to a discussion about ordination. This dance was present in the colloquium as well, which displayed varying levels of comfort in discussing ordination while maintaining incredibly strong critiques of abuses of power in the Church and denial of autonomy and the sacred personhood of African women.

I left the colloquium feeling both inspired and insignificant, needing to reflect on my own ministry as an advocate for women's ordination. Momentarily, I fell prey to a common criticism that women's ordination is disconnected from the praxis and immediacy of some of the life-threatening realities women face around the world. Sometimes that felt true. Is there revolution in the daily mechanics of running a nonprofit organization with what we know of poverty, violence, and war?

Having attended many gatherings and committee meetings of tired feminists, disenfranchised theologians, and underfinanced non-profiteers, the pioneering spirit and immediacy of the women's cau-cus and the energy of the group gathered there seemed somehow more alive. I even surprised myself in thinking, for perhaps the first time, that Catholicism seemed like a viable avenue for education, resources, and empowerment, even for women. It is as the sister said: the church is still oppressive, still in crisis, still perpetuating systemic injustices, but paradoxically a nucleus of change in this landscape. I felt proud to be part of a global church: something that connected me to these women and these forces of change.

In the 1970s in the United States, the women's ordination movement had a similar energy as a horizon of possibility. WOC published a monthly newsletter to its thousands of members; delega-tions met with the US Conference of Bishops' Committee on Women in Society and Church; Sr. Theresa Kane respectfully challenged the Pope directly on "ministerial equality"; and in the era of the Equal Rights Amendment, WOC members took to the media and the streets to make their voices heard. The creativity and passion of WOC's cam-paigns—both national and individual—poised a generation to believe and prepare for the day women would be welcomed in the

Catholic Church as priests. The endurance needed for a generation built on what felt like unstoppable momentum would ask too much of many of these women and men.

Indeed, after holding a torch to the patriarchy for more than forty years, muscles give out along with one's hope. I formally entered the women's ordination movement in a time when Pope Benedict XVI offered a perfect target for decades of disappointment and anger. For a revolution in a dark time—for feminists and for many Catholics—this was a "burn it down" stage. One of my favorite Italian theologians, Marinella Perroni describes a hermeneutic duality in facing change in the Catholic Church as between "resistance" and "resilience."[1] With resistance, we must challenge and reject that which does not serve the Gospel message of equality. Sometimes, resistance is an act of self-preservation; sometimes, it is running up against a brick wall. With resilience, we find ways to cope with the emotional and psychological trauma and stress of systemic oppression.

In any social movement, both resistance and resilience are necessary. In a global Church with no clear mechanism for change and brick walls imbued with a centuries-old cement of patriarchy and misogyny, the revolution must come from all sides, in extremes. I am often asked about our "strategy" for women's ordination: "How would it happen?" Barriers such as culture, Vatican documents, canon law, doctrine (according to some opinions), and the kind of exceptionalism that religions and the Holy See enjoy around the world in national and international law each present their own challenges and own entry points.

In recovering from my own feeling of smallness and scattering of priorities, I have to return to the simple ways God is present and found. As Dorothy Day wrote, "a pebble cast into a pond causes ripples that spread in all directions."[2] The work for women's ordination

[1] Kate McElwee, "'Resistance' and "Resilience' with Marinella Perroni," *The Table*, February 4, 2015, http://www.womensordination.org/blog/2015/02/04/resistance-and-resilience-with-marinella-perroni/.
[2] Dorothy Day, "Love Is the Measure," *Catholic Worker*, June 1946, 2.

is not simply about making women priests but also about connecting the inequality of women in the Church—knowing its influence around the world—to contributing and perpetuating a patriarchal culture that violates and oppresses women and girls to the point of violence and economic and social poverty. The intention behind the small daily work, creating spaces for women to safely gather and claim Catholic feminist ministry, is in its own way a caucus, a colloquium, a revolution.

I must believe in the extremes—the chipping away and the bulldozing. The revolution must be both in the grandmother baptizing her grandchild, and in the chaos of stopping traffic on *via della Conciliazione*. I believe the revolution is plodding and personal, isolating and deafeningly quiet. It is she who rings the bell at the door of the Congregation of the Doctrine of the Faith and declares she has an appointment, and she who quietly breaks up with a white, male God.

The revolution is the cacophony of the people of God, each with an individual experience of God and still a chorus of hearts and minds who find meaning in a shared language and ritual. The revolution is a group of women gathering in the corner of a Jesuit college cafeteria in Nairobi sharing email addresses. It is those same women, earning their first and second doctorate degrees and publishing narrative theologies from the stories of the girls of Kibera. I believe God has chosen to need us, each of us, on this journey.

Pope Francis has said that our faith is revolutionary because it challenges dominant systems. The radical inclusion modeled by Jesus and the early Christian communities call all Christians to know God through the love and service of others, to work for the equality we know through our baptism, and to advocate for justice for the most marginalized by society. I am again reminded of a presentation at the colloquium that called for our faith institutions to be outraged, to cry out with us in our pain. The work for women's equality in the Catholic Church is about not only correcting an injustice in our church but also modeling equality in society. If we look to our Christian faith for our model of social justice, we must begin with such collaboration.

Our Vatican II documents claim "every kind of social or cultural discrimination in basic personal rights on the grounds of sex, race, color, social conditions, language, or religion" to be "incompatible with God's design."[3] Moreover, when the US bishops can declare "with certainty" that "discrimination against women contradicts the will of Christ," one might conclude radical feminism is written into our faith.[4] Catholics are called to be revolutionary in every instance of discrimination and injustice, to be humble and of service, resilient and resistant in the face of any system of oppression.

In our "universal call to holiness,"[5] Pope Francis has said, "we are all called to be saints . . . not just those who have the opportunity to break away from the ordinary tasks . . . Indeed, it is by living with love and offering Christian witness in our daily tasks that we are called to become saints . . . Always and everywhere you can become a saint, that is, by being receptive to the grace that is working in us and leads us to holiness."[6] For women's ordination activists, this echoes what we have known: the big and small, the quiet and loud, the daily witness for equality is our grace, our faith, and our revolution.

[3] Pope Paul VI, "Pastoral Constitution on the Church in the Modern World *Gaudium Et Spes*," December 7, 1965, http://www.vatican.va/archive/hist_councils/ii_vatican_council/documents/vat-ii_cons_19651207_gaudium-et-spes_en.html

[4] US Conference of Bishops, "Strengthening the Bonds of Peace: A Pastoral Reflection on Women in the Church and in Society," 1994 (usccb.org).

[5] Pope Paul VI, "Dogmatic Constitution on the Church, *Lumen Gentium*," November 21, 1964," http://www.vatican.va/archive/hist_councils/ii_vatican_council/documents/vat-ii_const_19641121_lumen-gentium_en.html.

[6] Emer McCarthy, "Pope at Audience: The Universal Call to Holiness"," *Radio Vaticana*, November 19, 2014, http://en.radiovaticana.va/news/2014/11/19/pope_at_audience_the_universal_call_to_holiness/1111603.

CHAPTER 7

## Mormon Feminism: Embracing Our Past, Envisioning Our Future

Caroline Kline

Fifteen years ago, a conversation with my then-boyfriend turned to the Mormon ideal of husbands presiding over wives. I couldn't understand why such language was necessary in what should be a relationship of equals. My boyfriend speculated, among other things, that it might simply mean that the man was ultimately more responsible for the family's success than the woman.

We explored that idea for a bit, but the more we talked about it, the sicker and more alone I felt. None of my other Mormon friends had ever questioned this ideal of husbands presiding, but the very idea that men should be preeminent or ultimately responsible was deeply troubling to me. As this dark feeling came over me, I first articulated to myself a truth I would later return to often: I am fully human, fully responsible before God, an agent in my own right, and an equal partner in the truest sense of the word. My future husband would need to see me as such for any marriage to survive. And God must see me as such as well.

As a person who insists on the inherent equality of men and women, I continue to question women's place in Mormon theology and the structural organization of the church. Thankfully, I have found in that boyfriend a husband who regards me as an equal partner, but women's subordinate position in the Church of Jesus Christ of Latter-day Saints (LDS) and some of its teachings is something that, unlike my marriage, I cannot easily reformulate. I admit that I want change.

Several of my non-Mormon friends have gazed at me with bafflement, asking why I don't just leave my patriarchal, conservative church. How do I explain the audacious, expansive beauty of some Mormon teachings? Despite the pain I feel at women's subordination in the church, I am drawn to Mormon ideas of every human's divine potential. I am inspired by the teachings of a God whose ultimate goal is that humans become God's eternal peers in the afterlife, not underlings. I love the Mormon conception of Eve as an insightful, courageous woman who dared to step forward and propel humankind on its cosmic journey toward divinity. I treasure Mormon beliefs in Heavenly Mother, the divine embodied consort of Heavenly Father. There is great feminist potential within Mormon teachings, but far too often, it is muted by androcentric and patriarchal teachings and practices that simultaneously subordinate and marginalize women.

My non-Mormon feminist friends recognize the constraints and limitations I confront as a woman in the Mormon Church, but do they recognize the good there is in the church? How do I explain the kind hearts of so many Mormons in my congregation? These are people who take their lives and choices seriously, who try so hard to be good, who are willing to drop their activities at a moment's notice if they find out someone needs help, and who are often willing to embrace and support even those like myself, who openly identify as feminist and liberal—a strange and baffling choice to many of them.

It's not always easy to hold together these two identities I so fiercely cling to—Mormon and feminist. At times, I feel like they will claw me apart. But then I remember my powerful Mormon foremothers in Utah, who fought tirelessly for suffrage in the nineteenth century, becoming the first women in the country to exercise the right to vote in 1870, fifty years before the Nineteenth Amendment passed. These ardently independent women often experienced boundless misery within their polygamous marriages, but their commitment to women and women's rights was unbounded. They published one of the first feminist newspapers in the nation, the *Woman's Exponent*, which brandished the tagline, "The Rights of the Women of Zion, and the Rights of the Women of all Nations." These were women deeply engaged in the issues of their times, who envisioned women rising up to stand as equals with men. "Woman, 'rise! thy penance o'er, Sit thou in the dust no more; Seize the scepter, hold the van, Equal with thy brother, man," they would sing as they organized collectively for women's rights.[1]

These women inspire me to continue trying to hold my divided identity together. Ten years ago, when online forums were springing up to host Mormons' desire for further conversation and reflection on Mormon topics, I cofounded *The Exponent* (www.the-exponent.com), a Mormon feminist blog dedicated to featuring the thoughts, angst, ideas, and hopes of Mormon women likewise grappling with the position of women in the LDS faith. Women's voices, stories, and ideas may be nearly nonexistent in our Mormon lesson manuals, sermons, and other authoritative discourse, but at *The Exponent*, they take center stage. Women here find community and conversation, as well as a connection to Mormon feminist history, which included the first feminist wave during the suffrage movement and the second wave in the 1970s and 1980s, when a group of Mormon women decided to publish their own Mormon feminist newspaper, *Exponent II*, in honor of the original feminist publication. In this online forum, I found the community for which I had yearned, a community willing to delve into the most difficult topics related to Mormon gender ideals and expectations. Finally, I wasn't alone with my questions and my pain.

*The Exponent* was neither the first Mormon feminist blog nor the biggest—that honor goes to the wonderful *Feminist Mormon Housewives* (www.feministmormonhousewives.org), whose original tagline,

---

[1] The *Woman's Exponent* was published from 1872–1914 in Salt Lake City. *Exponent II*, a quarterly publication founded by Claudia Bushman and Laurel Thatcher Ulrich, and *The Exponent Blog*, founded by Caroline Kline, continue the original efforts of the *Woman's Exponent*.

"Angry activists with diapers to change," sums up its fabulousness—but it has been important. Because our church lesson manuals are overwhelmingly androcentric, we publish (among other content) feminist lesson plans, replete with thoughtful, progressive questions, a gender focus, and authoritative quotations from women. Every month, these lesson-plan posts receive tens of thousands of hits from Mormon teachers over the world looking for ideas for their Sunday lessons. Overall, *The Exponent* averages approximately sixty thousand hits per month, with the most popular posts featuring scores of comments by Mormons eager to speak openly about issues of gender. For many, the blog has been their gateway to feminism. For me, the blog has given me my most intimate friendships.

Over the years, my online connections have become real-life, life-changing relationships, and at times when I might have felt utterly alone in my questions or pain, I have had the blog and blogging friends to turn to for support and advice. I'll never forget the day when I didn't know whether I should move forward with holding my infant son in our Sunday service for his baby blessing, given my bishop's disapproval and strong advice that I not. (Traditionally, Mormon baby blessings consist of the father and other male friends and relatives holding and encircling the baby to pronounce a blessing.) Feeling discouraged, I turned to my blog friends for advice, and within an hour, I had twenty messages telling me to move forward, to think of what I would wish I had done when I look back on my life, and to push past my fear and hold my child. With their support, I gathered up my courage and did so. This is one very important thing the blog has given me and others—beloved friends who are there to make us strong when we are weak and discouraged.

To stand against the nearly overwhelming tide of conservative Mormon custom and expectation, women like myself have needed these Mormon feminist organizations and forums. Through our associations with each other, we have found new ways to visualize our religion and practice and the courage to act on these new visions. Determined to follow our consciences and despite fear of ecclesiastical discipline by Mormon leaders, some Mormon feminists are pushing against gender boundaries by creating our own religious rituals to lay hands on and bless our children and each other. While many of these blessings take place in women-only gatherings, women are starting to write publicly about these rituals on Mormon feminist blogs. They are claiming their power, their right to insert themselves into ritual territory considered male-only within Mormonism. In doing so, they are risking their own standing in their Mormon communities, since such action is considered strongly taboo and even heretical.

*The Exponent* blogger Meghan Raynes has poignantly discussed such a moment in her own life when her female friends, probably for the first time in their lives, crossed this boundary to reach out, lay hands on, and bless her as she was suffering a depressive episode. "This blessing was my life raft. I was drowning and these women used the power of God in every sense of what that means to save me. I was healed . . . and it was all because these wonderful women stood up against everything they were ever taught about authority and power and rejected it," Raynes wrote in *The Exponent* on November 6, 2011, in a post titled "Now I Have the Power."

I, too, have experienced the awesome power of beloved female friends encircling me and my baby and raining down blessings on our heads. Such experiences of women daring to venture into Mormon male ritual territory have emboldened me to free myself from other Mormon religious practices that sideline women. Over the last couple of years, I have occasionally modeled for my children inclusive prayer practices, addressing both Heavenly Mother and Heavenly Father. This goes against authoritative instruction from our Mormon male General Authorities who insist that prayers should be addressed to Heavenly Father. But ultimately, I knew I had to provide another model of prayer to my children, particularly my daughter. As my children develop their own spiritual identities, they will know alternative practices. And when my daughter feels erased and marginalized, she will recall that subversive memory of her own mother reaching up to female divinity in supplication.

Pressing the institution to move forward on issues of gender is important, but I also feel that it is important to authorize ourselves personally to move forward, reach out to divinity, and establish new patterns, rhetoric, and practice from the ground up. The institutional church will do what it will do, but I feel the pressing need to live my life, follow conscience, and model inclusive and generous spiritual practice to my children.

This truth came to me forcefully in fall 2015 when the LDS headquarters issued a new policy stating that same-sex marriage is an act of apostasy that mandates a church disciplinary council. Equally shocking, they have determined not to baptize the children of LGBTQ Mormons who are in same-sex relationships until the children are adults and renounce their parents' relationship. Sometimes, I despair of the Mormon institutional church—it seems as if it has boundless power to hurt those who should be treated most gently and lovingly. I immediately wrote letters of protest to church leaders, contacted an LGBTQ Mormon group, and offered to support them and their members in any way I could. In the coming months, I plan to host a support group for LGBTQ Mormons in my home. The institutional church will do what it will do, I tell myself again and again, as I fight back tears. And I will do what I feel I must do. It will not define me, my actions, or my Mormon identity.

When such tragedies are wrought by our institutional church, my Mormon feminist friends and I wrap our arms around each other—both in person and online—and cry. And then we write, write, and write more, so that others will know they are not alone with their questions or pain, so that others will know our empowering Mormon feminist past, so that others will know that there are expansive and inclusive alternatives within this endlessly complicated, rich, and bewildering tradition.

CHAPTER 8

# *Reproducing Justice*
## Kate Ott

C hristian faith communities, including my own Roman Catholic tradition, have historically been champions of justice as well as the purveyors of grave injustices. By coming to terms with this complex history, I came to understand that loving a faith tradition often means needing to speak out against it.

For me, growing up Roman Catholic was a source of pride and confusion. In my middle and high school years, I realized we were to feed the hungry, clothe the naked, and aid the sick but never raise questions about gender or sexuality. Why was there controversy over the girl altar servers? Why were only the boys questioned about their future careers and encouraged to participate in Church leadership? Why were girls to guard themselves from sex and protect their virginity from boys? How come there were so few scripture lessons about women? Why couldn't women be ordained? The deepest and most meaningful parts of my Catholic faith experience—service to those in need, community building, and rigorous education—seemed to be in opposition to what was being promoted related to sexuality and gender. What I hadn't realized was that asking too many questions and not accepting the prescribed answers would push me further from the institutional church and deeper into theological snares.

As I studied more and moved further to the margins of Roman Catholic communities, I found that sexuality and gender raised very volatile issues that could not be resolved. Love, it seemed, was not simple, nor were the relationships that surrounded it. My questions became more complex, mostly in response to the suffering and pain I witnessed within my family and by my friends; family structures challenged by interracial dating, a son or daughter coming out as gay, out-of-wedlock pregnancies, and abortion. I realized I had only imprecise language and categories, limited by what the Roman Catholic Church had provided, for my questions regarding sexuality, gender, relationships, and so on. It was as if sexuality was a trap and no one I knew could escape being a sinner in the eyes of the Church.

In my own faith development, I began to recognize how Church doctrines about family and marriage perpetuated exclusion, shame, and gendered double standards. In college, conversations in women and gender studies helped me uncover systemic sexism and its relationship to other oppressions like racism and classism. I learned about my own privilege as well as the damages I had suffered to my body image and self-confidence as a woman. Yet, feminism without religion felt like living free in a foreign land—exciting, eye-opening, and not quite right. Then, I found feminist theology and ethics. These writings respond to the very same issues I found myself struggling to reconcile. They uncover the intersections of religious patriarchy and systemic oppression in an effort to identify liberatory needs in our current world. They often compare the lived reality of the faithful and the power of the church hierarchy to show the diversity and struggle of living out faith values in an institutional religion while also creating new spaces for reinterpretation of harmful teachings. Some make arguments on behalf of women's ordination. Others offer feminist interpretations of the Bible, including outright condemnation of those passages that are death-dealing to women. Still others concentrate on engaging the sexual ethics of the hierarchy and making room for women's lived experiences as resources for theological reflection.

Indeed, much of my personal experience has helped me better understand the everyday sexuality and reproductive health struggles that women of faith face. Months into my marriage and the start of my theological education, I became pregnant. Twenty weeks into the pregnancy, we were given a diagnosis of abnormal development and fetal demise. After a battery of tests, we had three options: abortion by dilation and curettage, abortion by inducing early delivery, or just waiting for fetal death to occur and risking toxicity to my body. Not only was I emotionally blindsided but I was morally torn. I supported better access to health care, sexuality education, and antipoverty initiatives to help reduce teen pregnancy but didn't think mothers who intentionally became pregnant faced abortion decisions. To be handed a piece of paper that read "Sign here: I agree to have an abortion" shook me theologically.

In my soul-searching discernment, I had many conversations with my husband, friends, and Roman Catholic spiritual advisors. These advisors told me the truth about the Church's teaching. They told me that the final choice was mine and should be based on my conscience. That no priest or religious leader could know what was in my conscience and that Church teachings had developed over time and always needed to be put into pastoral context to promote the flourishing of humanity not the destruction or harm of lives and relationships. I knew what had to be done in order to bring closure, dignity, and safety. I signed the paper and consented to abortion.

I know this story can be seen as one of the medical reasons for abortion that people dismiss as "not what they are talking about" when it comes to abortion debates. Some will claim it was not actually abortion because the procedure was aiming at saving my life and preserving the dignity of the fetus. Whatever rhetorical hoops we jump through, the reality is not all abortions are the same. Regardless, we should always trust women's moral agency to make such decisions. The Roman Catholic tradition values conscience in moral decision making. Conscience is not a "gut reaction"; conscience is well formed through relationship and personal experience and informed by Church teachings and wider bodies of knowledge. The Church says that we are required to follow our conscience, first and foremost in moral decisions. Had I not learned about the Catholic tradition of conscience and had faithful guides to assist me in forming my decision, I would have thought the Church disowned me. I grieved the loss of that pregnancy, but never once have I felt that God did not support me in my decision. Loving oneself as one's neighbor often makes for very complex moral decisions. Many women face a similar decision, often without the same access to health care or relational support that I had, believing their faith communities will condemn and expel them. Women deserve to be valued equally to men in their ability to make moral decisions in the best interest of their lives and that of their current and future families.

The many lives I have seen damaged directly by Church teachings on sexuality as well as those indirectly harmed by lack of sexuality education or reproductive health services motivate my advocacy, as does my own personal experience. In the moments when my and other's human dignity and moral worth are questioned—because of gender or sexual orientation or use of a condom to prevent pregnancy and the spread of STDs—I get angry. Even though I feel these issues personally, these aren't issues only about *some* people—how we form our families; what options we have to plan pregnancies; the opportunity to love mutually and safely; that our bodies should be respected and our health needs cared for—these are everyone's issues. Roman Catholic political influence in the United States, not to mention globally, perpetuates injustices based on sexuality and gender related to health care access, comprehensive sexuality education for youth, and legal rights and protections for gay, lesbian, and transgender (LGBT) people. In fact, the majority of Catholics in the United States neither agree with nor follow the teachings of the hierarchy when it comes to issues related to sexuality. For example, the majority of Catholics in the United States support women's ordination, same-sex marriage, access to/use of contraception, making abortion legal in all or most cases, divorce and remarriage, and LGBT nondiscrimination laws, and oppose sweeping religious liberty exemptions.[27] Over time,

---

[1] See Public Religion Research Institute, "The Francis Effect? U.S. Catholic Attitudes on Pope Francis, the Catholic Church, and American Politics," August 25, 2015, http://publicreligion.org/research/ 2015/08/survey-the-francis-effect-u-s-catholic-atti-tudes-on-pope-francis-the-catholic-church-and-american-politics/#.VeWou_IVjCo; and Jen Girdish, "Future Church: New Polling on Catholic Millennials," *Conscience* 36, no. 1 (2015): 14–19.

small dismissals of questions, quiet shunning of Church members, and large-scale repetition of ecclesiastical power breeds frustration and often anger. The majority of Catholics suggest that the Church focus its energies on social justice work such as ending poverty. Consider the difference that could be made if the US bishops redirected the excessive dollars spent on lobbying related to restricting reproductive health care access on the basis of religious liberty to antipoverty initiatives.

As Beverly Wildung Harrison wrote in her now infamous inaugural lecture as the first woman appointed to the Christian ethics professorship at Union Theological Seminary,

> Anger is not the opposite of love. It is better understood as a feeling-signal that all is not well in our relation to other persons or groups to the world around us. Anger is a mode of connectedness to others and it is always a vivid form of caring. To put the point another way: anger is—and it always is—a sign of some resistance in ourselves to the moral quality of the social relations in which we are immersed.[2]

In this lecture, Harrison was responding to the patriarchy that deforms the Christian tradition and our society. She was also arguing that feelings arise as part of our moral action. They themselves are not moral acts but help us discern how to move toward moral action. To put my anger to use in the work of love, I join feminist colleagues, teachers, and pastors who help young people think through sexuality issues in an open, honest, and faith-based manner as well as advocate out of my faith values for access to reproductive health services. It saddens me to hear that some came to know their sexualities, found good relationships, or planned their families *in*

---

[2] Beverly Wildung Harrison, "The Power of Anger in the Work of Love: Christian Ethics for Women and Other Strangers," in *Making the Connections: Essays in Feminist Social Ethics*, ed. Carol S. Robb (Boston, MA: Beacon, 1985), 14.

*spite of* their faith tradition. I want them to know their sexuality as good and find life-affirming relationships *because* of what the Christian, and even Catholic, faith tradition has to offer.

I join many of the faithful in advocating for doctrinal changes regarding women's ordination, marriage equality, and reproductive justice in the Roman Catholic Church. I am not as active as many others. Such creative, vocal, tireless activists live out the best of what sainthood is: the gospel message of residing with the least among us; standing up to political and institutional powers fueled by their relationship with God; and creating community through common witness to God's immediate work in the world. My contribution is slightly different. I am thankful for the opportunity to have written the book *Sex + Faith: Talking to Your Child from Birth to Adolescence.* The book and workshops I lead invite Christians to ask: How do my faith values influence how I treat my children or my spouse? Does the love we nurture and the way we value our bodies lead to treating others with dignity and respect? Do the friendships we have challenge us to move beyond our sameness? Does the sexuality education our faith community provides encourage healthy development and faith connections or silence and shame? How we love at home is not simply a personal choice: it has communal impacts that can either reify existing sinful structures or disrupt them. To love God and to love our neighbors as ourselves is revolutionary work that can start at home!

I became a Christian ethics professor and a faith-based sexuality educator on account of a mix of chance, calling, and determination. My experiences taught me that the overwhelming, broad nature of oppressions like racism and sexism can leave us feeling guilt ridden and inadequate to make change. However, the all-encompassing nature of evil and systemic sin is not invincible if we are able to admit that our everyday interactions sustain it. Working consistently through our interpersonal relationships, we can slowly dismantle the hold that such evils have in our lives. In addition to parent and youth education, I spend much of my time educating clergy in professional sexual ethics. Better prepared clergy will hopefully lead to decreases in sexual misconduct, implementation of holistic faith-based sexuality education, and more compassionate pastoral care. To provide safety and information to a woman seeking answers about her sexuality and taking responsibility for reproductive choice, to be with a couple as their mutual love is affirmed regardless of their gender, to help a teenager value her body in all its diversity as part of God's creation—these are acts of love and education that start small, lasting revolutions in people's lives.

# CHAPTER 9

## *Pregnant with Sacred Truth*

### Katey Zeh

For the last half hour I have been sitting at my desk, staring intently at my pregnant belly as it jumps, wiggles, and shifts in an awkward, uncoordinated dance. I am completely fascinated by it. Even when I am in a state of total concentration, as soon as this movement begins, I instantly lose all focus on the task at hand. While this might sound like an inconvenient or even annoying distraction, for me it serves as a constant reminder of why I advocate for health, rights, and justice for women and girls.

My experience of pregnancy has revealed to me just how much privilege I enjoy as an educated white woman with economic means. To start, I have never had to worry about access to things I need, like top-notch prenatal care, healthy food, and prenatal vitamins. But my privilege is about so much more than my ability to meet these basic needs; it is something that I *embody*. When I go out to walk my dog or run to the grocery store, strangers take in my swollen belly and smile because I meet our culture's narrowly defined set of criteria for an acceptable pregnancy. Married to a man? Check. Not too young or old? Check. Financially stable? Check. Simply put, I got pregnant the "right" way.

The "right" way was something I learned all about as an adolescent in an evangelical United Methodist congregation in southeast Georgia. Most of my peers were baptized as babies and attended Sunday school every week, but my immediate family did not participate in any kind of organized religion. Around age eight I decided on my own to go to church with my terminally ill grandmother. Attending worship was a way to spend time alone with her, and after she died, it was my connection to her memory. One of the things she left me was a book about the life of Jesus; it fascinated me. I had never heard of his miracles, his death, and his resurrection. My curiosity about Jesus piqued, I asked my mom for a Bible (we did not have one in our house) and permission to go to church camp. Before long, I had happily and completely absorbed the evangelical culture that dominated the religious landscape of my small hometown.

Church was a place of belonging, something I desperately wanted as a kid whose parents were divorcing, even if that belonging meant sometimes going along with rules and ideas that didn't make sense to me. Around the time I entered middle school, I began attending a weekly youth group at a friend's church, mostly because it involved free pizza and socializing without many rules. I was not much of a rebellious spirit, but because my family was not part of the community, youth group was an outlet for experimenting with just what kind of teenager I wanted to be. Little did I know my youth group leaders had other ideas. When I was in eighth grade, the new-at-the-time True Love Waits sexual abstinence curriculum became a focus of our youth-group gatherings. The leaders told us that part of our identity as Christians was strict adherence to the rules set before us regarding sexuality. At age thirteen, I naïvely took a purity pledge, driven mostly by peer pressure and lacking any real understanding of what my commitment meant—or how it connected to Jesus's example of love, grace, and acceptance in the Gospels.

These abstinence teachings placed disproportionate responsibility on young girls to maintain them, and so I had grown more suspicious of them by the time I was in my late teens. One particularly telling moment was at a girls' Bible study where I first heard the phrase "keep the bow on the package." This seemingly cutesy phrase sent a very clear, direct message: we were to remain sexually pure so that on our wedding night, our husbands could fully enjoy the gift of our virginity. The assumption was that if we put our sexuality on hold, we would each be rewarded with a husband and, presumably, a healthy, happy marriage. Looking back, I suppose this was meant to motivate us, but at seventeen years old, I was focused on college applications not the possibility of a husband. All I heard in "keep the bow on the package" was judgment and blame.

In the evangelical circles I grew up in, people often talked about the moment when they "got saved." I have my own conversion story, but it looks quite different from those I heard as a young person. During my sophomore year at Davidson College, I enrolled in a theology seminar that dedicated an entire class to Valerie Saiving's groundbreaking essay "The Human Situation: A Feminine View" in which she challenges Reinhold Niebuhr's position that all sin is rooted in self-centeredness and that love, as embodied by Christ, is self-sacrificial.[1] She explores the idea that sacrificing oneself can be sinful when a person identifies too closely with another and loses her sense of self. Most notably, she speaks of motherhood as a time when many women commit the "sin" of losing themselves.

It was as if my world had been turned upside down. Reading these words was a jolt to my belief system. Suddenly, all that I had been taught in church about who I was supposed to be—submissive, obedient, even self-deprecating—was revealed to be a complete distortion of the Christian story! In fact, that worldview was inherently *sinful*. When I denied my selfhood, I also denied my sacred worth as a child of God. Saiving's words opened up new spaces in my spirit for understanding the divine in ways I had never encountered—as a mother, as holy mystery, as the source of life. From that point on, I claimed feminist theology as a source of sacred truth and dedicated my studies and spiritual growth to learning this new faith language.

Feminist theology called into question nearly all of the messages about faith I had received up until that point, but it completely

---

[1] Valerie Saiving Goldstein, "The Human Situation: A Feminine View," *Journal of Religion* 40, no. 2 (1960): 100–11.

deconstructed the idolization of female sexual abstinence that was so emphasized during my teen years. I witnessed how even the strictest adherence to the standards of sexual purity failed miserably when it came to ensuring a marriage was healthy, happy, and fulfilling. Several of my friends who had remained virgins until their wedding nights were in the middle of painful divorces that led to their crises of faith: how could this be happening when they had done everything the "right" way?

I spent my fair share of time feeling deep bitterness and anger toward the religious leaders and community of faith that had led all of us so far astray. No church felt like a safe place to me. When I did attend a worship service, I was on high alert for sexist practices like the use of exclusive male language for God, which seemed to dominate every community I visited. I would leave feeling drained and even more convinced that there was no hope for me in finding a community where I would find shared values.

But what I lost in the faith community, I found again in my evolving understanding of the divine as the one who embraces all beings, who calls each of us beloved and good, and whose presence is within us all. No longer bound to the narrow theological teachings of my adolescence, I became increasingly comfortable with holy mystery. As I let go of the need I once had for straightforward answers to my questions about God, I began to imagine and experience the divine in new ways. All of the energy I once had expended to following rules, to going about my life in the "right" way, I now channeled into a spirit of openness and wonder. And God started showing up in places I least expected.

In line with my "conversion" to feminism, my story of call is not what I would consider traditional. For starters, it took place at the local Planned Parenthood clinic. I had taken a one-day course on pastoral care for women and couples facing difficult pregnancies and wanted to put my new skills to work. I signed up for shifts on an anonymous hotline that patients could call for support but decided I first needed to understand exactly what happened in the clinic setting. Up until then, I had never set foot in a Planned Parenthood clinic. Not because I had avoided doing so purposely, but because I had always had insurance and access to private medical care. Initially, I encountered some skepticism from the staff about exactly why a divinity school student would want to volunteer there. They were so accustomed to religious people antagonizing their patients and attacking their work, that it was hard for them to believe I was there to be supportive. But I shared with them that my faith called me to care for and stand alongside women making difficult decisions about their lives, including the decision to terminate a pregnancy.

Each week when I drove into the parking lot, I began to understand what daily life was like for the staff and patients. Religious protesters would stand on the sidewalk with outstretched arms, holding the antiabortion literature that they tried to offer me as I drove past. At first, the protesters assumed I was a patient and would yell at me as I made my way from my car to the door, "Don't kill your baby!" But after a few weeks, the protesters recognized that I was coming in regularly and changed their shouts to things like, "Blood is on your hands!" As resolved as I felt about the work I was there to do, I initially had a hard time completely resisting the onslaught of shame and guilt thrust upon me each time I made that short walk into the clinic.

What inspired me to return week after week was what I saw inside the clinic walls—doctors providing services with compassion and understanding for the women in their care, medical technicians speaking to each patient with kindness and respect, support staff working long hours to make sure every person received the services she needed. It occurred to me that while the visibly religious people were outside protesting, the real ministry of healing and hope was happening inside.

I might not have had the language to name it at the time, but my experience of volunteering at Planned Parenthood was when I received my call to work for reproductive justice. Suddenly, I had clarity; I could see a thread running through my life—from the purity messages I received as an adolescent to the angry, condemning cries of the people protesting at Planned Parenthood—of how often people distort religion into nothing more than a thinly veiled form of misogyny. For many, this is enough to write off religion altogether, but for me this was a catalyst for transformation. I knew that women

deserved better and that God had called me to more than simply surrendering to the status quo.

My commitment to reproductive health, rights, and justice is
theologically rooted in the divine truth that women and girls are children of God, with sacred worth. Perhaps this seems obvious, but
when we look at the myriad ways in which women are devalued,
marginalized, and objectified around the globe, this belief is, in fact,
quite controversial and countercultural. Throughout history and
today, women and girls have been reduced to their reproductive
organs, to be put on a pedestal, to be restricted, or to be condemned.
Tragically, faith communities are often the worst culprits of this collective sin. So often, I've encountered women and men who have
made difficult decisions about their health and families and feel they
cannot share their stories with anyone, especially not faith leaders, in
fear that they will be judged and condemned.

As a person of faith, I am called to sacred truth telling that invites
others into community with one another rather than contributes to the
increasingly vitriolic public discourse around abortion. Working for
reproductive freedom as a Christian is first and foremost about living
my life with compassion. Part of the privilege I carry with me is the freedom to tell my story, and I aim to do so in a way that shines a light on
issues that are not always named in the public square. For example, I
can share honestly about the struggles I have encountered in my own
planned, very wanted pregnancy and how that experience has moved
me to a place of even deeper compassion for those whose journeys are
much more troubled than my own. I often say, if this pregnancy is challenging for me, with all of the privilege I have, how much more challenging is it for those who lack access to care, resources, and support?

I am particularly grateful to the women of color leaders who
first coined the term *reproductive justice* and who continue to challenge
me with their words and their work.[2] As a privileged white feminist I

---

[2] See Loretta Ross, "Understanding Reproductive Justice: Transforming the Pro-
choice Movement," *off our backs* 36, no. 4 (April 2006) 14–19. The entire issue in
which her article appeared was dedicated to women of color and their defining of
the movement of reproductive justice.

must recognize that the movement is about much more than universal access to reproductive health care. These reproductive-justice leaders have shown me how oppressions intensify and magnify one another—how the intersections of gender, sexuality, race, class, and other are where we must seek greater understanding and systemic change. Through their teachings, I have learned how we must do much more than focus on individual decision making if we wish to create a world in which every person is truly free. This is the world that I want for my child.

I believe that through the transforming power of the Spirit, God invites us to be cocreators of a more just, compassionate world in which we are all free to live into our identities as children of God with sacred worth. I look to the ministry of Christ, who reached out with hands of healing and compassion, who saw women as full human beings worthy of his time and attention, and who came that all might experience abundant life here and now. His example is a challenge to us to live into the sacred truth that all of us—especially women and girls—are children of God. As I prepare to birth a new human life into this difficult, beautiful world, I hope for nothing less.

CHAPTER 10

## Shamed Bodies: Eating, Empathy, and Sisterhood as Spiritual Practices of Revolt
Stephanie N. Arel

P hysiologically and symbolically significant, food represents a source of life support and pleasure. Commonly associated with rituals—familial, cultural, and religious—the experience of eating connects the solitary act of food consumption with a world of meaning. But what happens internally around food, not biologically or physically but psychically? Our mental and affective experiences of eating fluctuate due to a variety of external factors. Many of the messages about food we hear are neither pleasant nor helpful. And while positive connotations and experiences of food exist, food can be a source of pain. Conversely, food, or its absence, can also anesthetize, interfering with our engagement with the world.

For three years, while I was studying for my bachelor's degree, I witnessed this phenomenon. I volunteered in a women's hospital that specialized in two distinct programs: birthing and eating disorders. When I arrived each night to work, I entered through the maternity ward. Happy families filled the entranceway. Babies' first cries accompanied me as I walked back to the eating-disorder unit, providing a contrast that I will never forget and which mirrors what I have come to understand as characterizing women's relationships to food. In this environment, scenes of joy and nourishment juxtaposed with moments of struggle and discord.

The dualities present in the women's hospital reflect a psychoanalytic dimension expressed in our encounters with food, encapsulated by the child's separation from its first food source: the mother, via breast or bottle.[1] The image of a mother feeding her child aligns food with nurturing. But as the baby's cry indicates, the sustenance provided by food through the mother exceeds its biologically necessary function. Being fed transforms into a sense of being loved, held, and comforted. However, when food becomes a source of psychic comfort, the act of eating becomes more than a physical requirement to fuel bodies. Subsequently, food affects us. Food interferes with our emotions, and to complicate matters, food always shows up on our bodies. Bodies mark the conspicuous intersection of food's conception as sustenance and our psychological negotiation with it. The bodies of the women in the eating-disorder unit varied in shape and size, but I was continually astounded by the reality that although their experiences with food differed—some women found food a friend, others an enemy to be thwarted—their deepest need, to be loved, was always the same.

Using food to experience love or to keep love at bay may appear illogical. But when we reflect on our habits with food, how we eat can often be connected to what we emotionally need at any given moment. Food consumption may also relate to our own early childhood experiences of love, not isolated from how we learn to love ourselves. The complication of how food manifests on our bodies creates an additional level of vulnerability because others can *see* how we experience food.

At the point of convergence, where food meets bodies, the feminist phrase "the personal is political" comes to fruition. When the personal act of eating involves how we look, a subject rife with implications related to women's position in society, the act of eating takes on political connotations. Thus, eating cannot be separated from how women participate in society. Food and women's bodies remain a focus of most media related to women's lives. Bodies serve as

---

[1] This situation is represented in the body of Melanie Klein's theory and work. See specifically, Klein, "Our Adult World and Its Roots in Infancy," *Human Relations* 12 (1959): 291–303.

the central point of critique for women in the public eye. The societal pressure to possess or seek a certain body type affects all of us. At its worst, the desire to measure up to standards placed on women's bodies leads to dangerous behaviors that occur around food consumption. At base, disordered eating represents a way to control something, some affect, and some part of us that feels dispossessed or uncontrollable. When our bodies continually function as loci of assessment, food represents a way of reclaiming power. But all too often that reclamation happens at our own expense, and our bodies suffer. The way that we eat can serve, however, as a means of refusing to allow the subsumption of our self-worth by ideal images of beauty projected by society. The way we eat can manifest as an act of self-love, refuting the shame that expectations about our bodies' appearance generate. When love of our bodies becomes a refusal to feel shamed about them, we enter into a mode of revolt that engenders in us the possibility for a new relationship with food, our bodies, and ourselves.

Eating appropriate foods and amounts of food is a form of self-care. Eating or drinking more or less than the body needs manifests as pleasure or abuse. Food deprivation or overeating illustrates a lack of compassion toward the self. At the extreme, such behaviors represent self-inflicted violence and thus evoke the need for treatment centers. Eating and consumption become a means of control—literally of rejecting or accepting claims made on the body. These claims echo as demands on the body's size and appearance.

For instance, the media—supported by patriarchal claims on women's bodies as objects of use whose value emerges depending on shape, size, age, color, and so on—supports the perpetual insanity around food in women's lives. In *The Beauty Myth*, Naomi Wolf referred to scholarship and research about beauty, deducing that the beauty of bodies is not about "evolution, sex, gender, aesthetics, or God" but rather about "emotional distance, politics, finance, and sexual repression."[2] She contended that rather than communicating what

---

[2] Naomi Wolf, *The Beauty Myth: How Images of Beauty Are Used against Women* (1991; repr., New York: Perennial, 2002), 13.

bodies should look like, the beauty myth is a form of social control. In this structure, ideals about beauty coerce women into unhealthy behavior. Wolf wrote, "the beauty myth is always actually prescribing behavior not appearance."[3] She introduced another problem inherent in the relationship with food and its implications on bodies: that how and what we eat, along with the layers of meaning that behaviors around food and bodies assume, threaten and disrupt female solidarity. "Competition between women," Wolf declared, has been made part of the beauty myth "so that women will be divided from one another."[4]

Wolf presented the problems of eating disorders as emerging from a dynamic of competition and self-hate, referring to the mind-numbing effects of anorexia as a disenabling of women's potential. Wolf named this a political problem because women suffering from eating disorders are "exhausted. And they're exhausted because they're starving or they're exhausted because they're vomiting compulsively."[5] The result of using or abusing food leaves us in a fog; as a result, according to Wolf, women's voices are "diminished; their reasoning powers are blunted."[6] When this happens, our thinking and leadership capacities are inhibited. Our self-worth diminishes and leaves us open to the detrimental effects of shame.

The *Diagnostic and Statistical Manual of Mental Disorders*, fifth edition (*DSM-5*), determines the diagnostic criteria and features, prevalence (anorexia and bulimia occur ten times more often in women's lives than in men's), development, risk and prognostic factors, culture-related diagnostics, and diagnostic markers for eating disorders.[7] Along with anorexia and bulimia nervosa, the *DSM-5* recognizes binge-eating disorder. Although diagnostic categories are rigid, a wide range of disordered eating habits emerges in these

---

[3] Ibid., 14.

[4] Ibid.

[5] Naomi Wolf, "Statement on Dying to Be Thin," *Gifts of Speech*, July 1997, http://gos.sbc.edu/w/wolf2.html.

[6] Ibid.

[7] American Psychiatric Association, *Diagnostic and Statistical Manual of Mental Disorders*, 5th ed. (Arlington, VA: American Psychiatric Publishing, 2013): 351–53.

classifications. Within these designations are important features including the affective associations with the disorders. For instance, the *DSM*-5 reports that individuals with bulimia, or binge eating, "are ashamed of eating problems and attempt to conceal their symptoms." Eating disordered behavior usually happens in secret or as "inconspicuously as possible," manifesting a desire to control the environment.[8] As with many experiences that are evident of pathology, as Helen Block Lewis asserts, shame is the "sleeper" effect.[9]

Feelings of shame around food and bodies, as Wolf intimated in her writings about the beauty myth, are not reserved for those with a clinical diagnosis. We experience shame when we believe our bodies are not good enough. And when we punish ourselves through food, shame increases, trapping us in a pernicious bind. This bind manifests psychoanalytically as repetition compulsion, repeating over and over again ritualized behaviors around food: overeating at a banquet table, promises of exercise that never occur, and purging by not eating for days or hours, exercising fanatically, or vomiting. These actions constitute ways we make ourselves sick with food. Rather than helping us manage whatever it is we attempt to control through food, we are left defeated, in shame. We find ourselves weighed down by the shame of bodies that are not good enough, compounded by the shame about the behaviors we engage in to avoid that shame in the first place.

The use of food as a response to shame represents a type of violence on the self. In such a way, disordered eating of any kind, any range, and at any rate of occurrence functions as a part of the shame cycle. The feeling of being out of control—related, for instance, to relationships, money, jobs, school expectations, or family situations—emerges in acts around food consumption. We feel embarrassed by our eating habits, and we hide them or talk about them

---

[8] Ibid., 351.
[9] Helen Block Lewis, "Introduction," in *The Role of Shame in Symptom Formation*, ed. Helen Block Lewis (London: Psychology Press, 1987).

incessantly as a way to mask the shame. In either case, we refute self-care when we allow food and messages about our bodies related to food to become an obsessive focus. Ultimately, we create distance between others and ourselves.

Obsessive or disordered eating represents hostility where aggression toward the self is followed by guilt, shame, and subsequent attempts at the inhibition of aggression. This may be marked by anger toward the self's failure—at "correcting" our bodies or failing again to eat "properly." This provokes a sense of helplessness, and the resulting passivity morphs into shame, which manifests as overcompensatory aggression and then further guilt.[10] Shame that is evoked but not repaired increases or maintains levels of symptomatic behavior.[11] Disordered eating is a symptom that sets up what Léon Wurmser calls the "the well-known endless sequence of shame about shame."[12] Shame looms in our relationship to food and our bodies. And since shame silences us, while also interfering with empathetic connections, our experiences of shame act effectively to socially control us.

Lorraine Caputo names shame as a central affect that disturbs our relationships with food and with each other, emphasizing that shame about bodies divides women from one another instead of connecting them.[13] Such behaviors form as an illness, and according to Ann Ulanov, "illness is exile."[14] An important complication of shame lies embedded in the ideas of division and exile: shame inhibits that which can repair it, empathic connection. Empathy, the experience of being able to imagine the emotions of another as well as share these, releases the detrimental grip of shame. In the naming

---

[10] Gerhart Piers and Milton B. Singer, *Shame and Guilt: A Psychoanalytic and Cultural Study* (New York: W. W. Norton, 1971), 32.

[11] Thomas J. Scheff, "The Shame-Rage Spiral: A Case Study of an Interminable Quarrel," in Lewis, *Role of Shame in Symptom Formation*, 109.

[12] Léon Wurmser, "Shame: The Veiled Companion of Narcissism," in *The Many Faces of Shame*, ed. Donald Nathanson (New York: Guilford, 1987), 80.

[13] Lorraine Caputo, "Gender, Food, and Loss," *Studies in Gender and Sexuality* 12, no. 3 (2011): 179–95, esp. 181 and 183.

[14] Ann Belford Ulanov, *The Unshuttered Heart: Opening Aliveness/Deadness in the Self* (Nashville, TN: Abingdon, 2007), 20.

and sharing of shame, women bond. This bonding emerges in the feminist idea of sisterhood, not as an individual pursuit or as an alternate version of an ideal but as a connection based on mutual interest. Such bonding emerges as women's refusal to participate in the dialect of shame and competition that keep us at odds. This refutation is both a spiritual and political action.

When we engage in food as a source of nurturing that allows us to live full lives and not as a means of body control, we begin to loosen the ties of competition that fester in our relationships to other women because we start to disempower shame. This is a spiritual practice. As a spiritual practice it cannot be, according to Nelle Morton, disassociated from political engagement. Morton writes, "*spiritual* is experienced as sisterhood in its loftiest and most universal sense and . . . political action of the most radical sort on behalf of and including all humanity—women, children, and men."[15]

Enjoying food and surrendering to the fact that we need food for sustenance, just as we need each other, takes practice. Refusing to allow societal messages about our bodies to continue to undercut our relationships with each other allows the bonds of sisterhood to grow. This is not an easy task. Disregarding the messages we are told about food and our bodies every day, and which continually operate to divide us, requires our persistent attention.

Issues around food—bodies, shame, and symbols—must be confronted. And while categories in the *DSM-5* may not apply to all or even many women, the experience of shame about both our bodies and our eating is something shared by all of us. The challenge to pull ourselves out of the ocean of doubt, shame, and insecurity about food and bodies, to refuse to play into the beauty myth, is a spiritual and political one. It takes incredible effort—or maybe some grace. For me, refuting messages that tell me the value of my self is predicated upon my body requires attention of the devotional sort, and examining this dynamic represents mobility toward activism. Working toward social and political change around food includes

---

[15] Nelle Morton, *The Journey Is Home* (Boston: Beacon, 1985), 98.

refusing the shame that alienates us from each other. It includes denying the beauty myth and rejecting competition that comes to us through a form of gross melding of our bodies into something particular and unachievable.

Part of my revolt is a radical willingness to face whatever lies in my path with honesty, but also while suspending judgment to see what obstacles and behaviors have to tell me—about others and myself. This entails denying the competition inherent in patriarchal conceptions of the relationships among women. On an individual level, fostering self-compassion is a first ingredient to being capable of really working toward true solidarity. This remains a constant root of my own spiritual and political praxis. On a social level, self-compassion enables a reaching out to the other, supporting a commitment to always work toward that which I think is the most helpful for all of humanity.

The most beautiful rituals that took place in the women's hospital occurred when patients prepared to go home. Those who remained assumed the task of conducting a formal farewell. Generally, this manifested as something creative. The women would perform a skit, throw a "birthday" party, or write a story and read it aloud. Whatever the method, the event evidenced the intense bonding that these women (and every so often, a man) experienced in their time together. They shared some of their deepest, most vulnerable parts of themselves and enjoyed love, some of them for the first time.

The formation of these kinds of relationships with other women solidified for me the concept that psychic gains to combat shame occur when shame is shared. This grappling with shame happened around food consumption: its interior representation and its social interpretation. These women also courageously negotiated their bodies, talking about what bodies represent socially and emotionally, while also disclosing how they abused their own and how they learned to care for them.

Through conversation and confrontation regarding the significance of having bodies as objects of scrutiny, their personal struggles translated into political resistance, and for me, they modeled a form of resistance. They exposed their bodies and their selves to each other to heal. Their restoration included engaging food differently— together they engaged in the radically intimate act of taking something into the body to nurture it. Eating for true nourishment and fostering empathic connections to disempower shame represent ways that we can revolt from the societal confines that entrap us. Engaging in practices to solidify bonds among women includes devotional practices of self-care that lead to our loving our bodies and ourselves.

Wolf encouraged us to believe that as women we are too precious to waste ourselves to the pursuit of an unhealthy, "anti-woman ideal."[16] Eating disorders are a form of revolt against the social control of the myth, but a better way to revolt exists. The revolution emerges in our connection to one another, in our making ourselves vulnerable, in sharing our shame, and in our refusal to allow shame about our bodies to dictate how we treat our bodies and ourselves. When we have the courage to say that the insanity around food and bodies that implores us to concentrate on ourselves to such an extreme that we lose sight of what we really need—healthy food and each other—we begin to loosen the coercive binds that keep us shackled, isolated, and in shame.

---

[16] Wolf, "Statement on Dying to Be Thin."

CHAPTER 11

# Firsthand Experience with Secondhand Shopping

Grace Y. Kao

A s someone who works as an ethicist, I have long appreciated various moral arguments for environmentalism and against unchecked consumerism. As a longtime Christian, I believe I have been called to live simply, in solidarity with all who bear the image of God and in good stewardship of all creation. However, upon becoming a first-time parent some seven years ago (now to two young boys), the need to leave the world a better place for future generations took on new significance and urgency. Fortunately for me, my identity as a feminist harmonized well with the direction toward which I was already being drawn for professional, religious, and familial reasons—to move with greater intensity in the direction of more sustainable living.

It hasn't been easy for me to counteract the bad habits I've accrued over a lifetime of living in a "throwaway culture" of convenience and overconsumption. While I am far from being an ecological moral exemplar, I have been more intentional in recent years about aligning my lifestyle, or daily habits of ordinary living, with the values I hold most dear.[1] Shopping at thrift stores instead of buying new has

---

[1] I had already been eating a primarily plant-based diet for most of my adult life for a host of environmental and other ethical reasons (for example, the fact that a mostly vegetarian diet uses significantly less of the earth's resources than a meat-based one and my desire not to be complicit in the agribusiness/meatpacking industry that exploits both the nonhuman animals to be slaughtered and the human workers tasked to do this difficult and dangerous labor).

accordingly become a regular way in which I live out some of my deepest feminist and Christian commitments.

One store. Thirty-five minutes. Two pairs of athletic shorts for my husband, four pairs of pants for my two boys, and one knit-jersey dress and two pairs of skinny pants for myself. $19.52 for the entire haul. All of this was possible simply by shopping secondhand.

There are many reasons why I—and many others like me—thrift, even if we can afford to shop elsewhere. First of all, thrift-store shopping is fun! It may be neither the most efficient nor the most pleasant way to shop—the stereotype of fluorescent lighting, musty smells, and racks overstuffed with product has some basis in truth. But I can usually spend less than forty-five minutes hunting for treasures in one store and emerge with several great finds. Thrifting encourages me to see the value in old things and even in styles of clothing, accessories, dishware, or other home goods toward which I wouldn't normally gravitate. That's an enjoyable kind of hunting expedition.

Buying clothes and other items secondhand is also a highly effective way to save money. To be sure, we are middle class and privileged enough to be able to afford to buy new at retail prices, but I love how I can regularly purchase items for all members of my household for a tiny fraction of what I would have had to pay at the mall, online, or even at a big-box, discount, or outlet store. Crucially, this means I can put the money I would otherwise have spent to other ends.

Beyond these (admittedly) self-serving reasons, thrifting is something I also do for the sake of the common good. Those of us who thrift follow the "reduce, reuse, recycle" mantra in this way: people donate clothes and other items they no longer need to thrift stores—thus decluttering their lives, which is a form of *reducing*. When folks like me buy secondhand, we are essentially *reusing* their castoffs and accordingly preventing them from clogging up our landfills. And the not insignificant portion of donated items that are not directly resold "as is" (either on-site or after exportation) is then *recycled* into wiping rags (for example, as industrial and residential absorbents) or converted into postconsumer fibers for home insulation and carpet padding and raw materials for the automotive industry.[2] The nonprofit Council for Textile Recycling estimates that through this reduce, reuse, recycle process, only 5 percent ends up as waste.[3] In essence, thrifting supports my ecofeminist and Christian convictions that we ought to live with greater awareness of the devastating environmental impact of human production, overconsumption, and waste, and accordingly, do what we can to shrink our ecological footprint.

Of course, thrift stores strengthen the bonds of community in still other ways. Beyond providing items at low prices for the indigent, most also have some sort of direct, charitable connection. For example, one of my favorite thrift stores, American Way (in Pomona, California), supports a charity for the blind; another that I frequent, Steven's Hope for Children (in Upland, California), provides financial assistance to the families of seriously ill or injured children who have relocated to be near a specialized hospital for treatment. Many of these thrift stores also provide vocational training or rehabilitation to persons on some form of state aid, including the developmentally disabled. Certainly, businesses that make it possible for persons of modest means to buy what they need, that contribute to charitable causes, and that treat adults with special needs with dignity as they train and employ them for work are ones that feminists or Christians committed to social justice should be inclined to support.

Besides those benefits, I admit I am also sickened by business as usual in the global retail apparel industry. Simply put, sweatshops, defined by the US Department of Labor as factories that violate two or more labor laws, are unfortunately behind the majority of clothes sold today.[4]  To be sure, the awfulness of sweatshops occasionally

---

[2] Council for Textile Recycling, "The Life Cycle of Secondhand Clothing," accessed April 8, 2016, http://www.weardonaterecycle.org/about/clothing-life-cycle.html. See also Sara Boboltz, "We Buy an Obscene Amount of Clothes. Here's What It's Doing to Secondhand Stores," *Huffington Post*, November 14, 2014.

[3] Council for Textile Recycling, "Life Cycle of Secondhand Clothing."

[4] To be sure, many antisweatshop activists will consider a factory a sweatshop even if it follows the "letter of the law" (which can be very weak in countries that attract sweatshops) but doesn't pay a living wage, offer safe working conditions, provide for sick or maternity leave, or allow workers to unionize (Green America, "Sweatshops," accessed October 1, 2015, http://www.greenamerica.org/programs/sweatshops/what-toknow.cfm).

makes front-page news—recall the media firestorm that ensued in the mid-1990s, when popular talk-show host Kathie Lee Gifford's Walmart clothing line was found to have been made by thirteen- and fourteen-year-old children working twenty-hour days in factories in Honduras, or more recently, when the Rana Plaza building in Bangladesh, which housed at least five garment factories, collapsed in May 2013, killing 1,137 people in the worst industrial accident in the history of the garment industry. But even as the general public learns about the harsh realities of sweatshops through these occasional news stories, I fear that most people nonetheless form the false impression that sweatshop conditions are the horrific *exception*—not the *norm*—in how clothes are being produced today.

But a damning April 2011 report by the International Textile Garment and Leather Worker's Federation (ITGLWF) suggests otherwise—the pervasiveness and normalcy of industry-wide labor abuses. Some sixty brands, ranging from high-end (think Calvin Klein, Nordstrom, Ralph Lauren, North Face, Tommy Hilfiger) to midrange (Abercrombie & Fitch, Adidas, Converse, Express, Levi's, Nike, GAP) to inexpensive or "fast fashion" (Forever 21, JC Penney, Old Navy, Walmart), were produced in eighty-three factories in Asia that violated numerous labor laws: most did not pay even the legal minimum wage, compelled workers to work excessive overtime without additional compensation, and physically or verbally intimidated or harassed workers when they failed to meet production goals.[5]

Most painful, to my mind, is the fact that sweatshop labor the world over is highly raced and gendered: 85 percent of sweatshop workers are young women of color between ages fifteen and twenty-five who either are desperately poor themselves working in developing countries or who are poor immigrants and/or undocumented workers in postindustrialized countries such as the United States. (Note that the "Made in the USA" label does not necessarily confirm the absence of sweatshop labor having been used to produce the

---

[5] For details, see Madeleine Bunting, "Sweatshops Are Still Supplying High Street Brands," *The Guardian*, April 28, 2011, http://www.theguardian.com/global-development/poverty-matters/2011/apr/28/ sweatshops-supplying-high-street-brands.

product.)[6] As corroborated by numerous antisweatshop advocates, a number of these factories force their mostly female labor force to take birth control or submit to routine pregnancy tests so they won't have to pay for maternity leave if the women become pregnant, and women who do are often then fired—in clear violation of domestic labor laws, human-rights standards, and (I would submit) common decency.

So when I turn *toward* thrift stores to meet my family's clothing wants and needs, the feminist and Christian in me are simultaneously attempting to turn *away* from an industry that routinely relies upon the exploitation of children and women. I simply don't want to be a part of a system that denies its workers what should be their right as a matter of course (like bathroom breaks) and thus don't want my purchasing habits to enrich those corporations that profit from the misery of those laborers.[7] When I additionally factor in the immense environmental impact of (new) clothing manufacturing today—cotton is the most pesticide-intensive crop in the world, nylon and polyester are nonbiodegradable, the process of bleaching and dying fabric is polluting and requires heavy water use—the burden on me either to make do and be content with what we have or to acquire things primarily by buying secondhand instead of new only increases.

While my initial forays some six years ago into thrift-store shopping were admittedly motivated by more self-interestedly practical than religious or ethical considerations, I now purchase almost all of my and my kids' clothes used, be they basics or seasonal items like Halloween costumes or wet suits, for principled reasons.[8] Of course,

---

6 "Feminists against Sweatshops," Feminist Majority Foundation, accessed October 1, 2015, http://www.feminist.org/other/sweatshops/ sweatfaq.html.
7 Of course, I could also—or instead—have adopted a strategy of buying new ethically produced clothes and other products from "green" businesses or those who abide by Fair Trade principles as set by the Fair Trade Federation and I commend those who do. But what tipped the scales for me in the direction of thrift-store shopping was the reality that manufacturing new products still almost always uses more of the earth's resources than does recycling goods that already exist and also because buying new doesn't usually carry the other ancillary benefits I previously mentioned.
8 Grace Kao, "Why I Thrift (and How I Got Started)," February 3, 2012, http://feminismandreligion.com/2012/02/03/why-i-thrift-and-how-i-got-started-by-grace-yia-hei-kao-2/.

thrifting per se is not inherently virtuous, as shoppers can still readily succumb to greed and materialism, given the lure of buying quality pieces at bargain prices. Nor does thrifting as a matter of course remove all complicity, since I do still buy new clothes for my family from time to time (underwear comes to mind) and am arguably still enjoying the fruits of exploitation when I thrift without paying the manufacturer's suggested prices for them. Thrifting can, however, reduce one's "formal cooperation with evil" (to use the technical vocabulary of Catholic moral reasoning) by requiring less of the earth's resources to sustain and by dramatically reducing the occasions by which an individual's procuring of adequate clothing must come at the expense of mostly poor, young, and nonwhite women toiling away in dismal conditions.

Thrifting for environmental and workers' rights reasons is an arena—and only one of many others—where my feminist and Christian commitments are mutually reinforcing, not in tension with each other. More specifically, feminism's slogan that the "personal is political" meshes well, in this case and others, with Christianity's focus on the cultivation of virtue (for example, stewardship, simplicity, and solidarity with the poor) in daily living through the discipline of repeated practices and habituation.

I am not deluded, however, into thinking that my private lifestyle choices (whether they be eating a largely plant-based diet or buying primarily secondhand rather than new) will themselves bring about systematic change. I do acknowledge that genuine transformation will require more than changing individual hearts and minds (and lifestyle choices)—it will also require real reform in institutions, laws, and policies through organized political activism and resistance. Thus, insofar as I actively both purchase at and donate to thrift stores, I do so in accordance with my conscience, and in solidarity with oppressed workers and in stewardship of the environment, but without duping myself into believing that my actions alone will usher in sweeping social change.

Still, the power of influence I have over those in my immediate sphere (and, of course, they over me) remains, as does the potential ripple effects of my actions upon others. In the same environmentalist spirit of reducing, reusing, and recycling, I am part of a circle of friends and colleagues who regularly exchange hand-me-downs, mostly in the form of children's clothing and toys. Thus, I continue to experience firsthand how sharing what we have not only enables us all to live more abundant lives but also strengthens our bonds of friendship and community.

I remember with fondness one time when I took my newly pregnant friend thrift-store shopping with me. I bought three cotton T-shirts for my then preschooler and a tunic-style top for myself and paid a grand total of $2.50. My friend, who hadn't thrifted in years but who ended up leaving with an impressive haul of her own, turned to me and said, "Wow, that's less than a latte." Indeed, she was right.

CHAPTER 12

## More Than Clothes Coming Off:
## Approaching Feminist Theology from the Strip Club

Betsy Coughlin

I only knew buildings with windows. For nineteen years, I made shadows in rooms that caught morning light and clutched it till sundown, rooms where the outside looked in and the inside looked out, curious about the other, but hardly crossing. Here's the trick that buildings with windows play: when I'm in them, it seems nothing separates me from outside—*me* from *them*; *me* from *you*. There is glass in-between; it buffers snow, hail, sleet, and wind. And glass dampens sounds of distress and abuse.

Those of us accustomed to buildings with windows scarcely notice buildings without, unless, of course, they are eyesores blighting an urban skyline. Those inside buildings without windows cannot reach out because there is no glass through which to see you. They do not know you are passing by. So it wasn't the sight of a building that interrupted my drive between Nashville and Jackson, Tennessee, but a bare, extended leg, wearing only an impossibly high heel that punched the sky across Interstate 40 in neon pink. "Gentleman's Club" shimmered and held the leg up, a letter or two flickering, soon to wink out. And just as I rolled by, the tip of that heel hooked me— hooked me and kindled a question: What goes on . . . no really, what goes on in there?

Those of us accustomed to buildings with windows are the ones whose figures make the shadows in a light-drenched room. We hardly know what it is to walk through spaces entirely shadowed, spaces where an unquenchable night is recreated starting at noon most days, including Christmas. There, in the darkness, we will never catch ourselves bouncing off the ground, our lines and curves mingling with sun.

My initial nudge toward the strip club is not the nudge that brings me back each week. When I first trailed that bare leg into the building without windows, I did so to turn the light on, bewitched by a vision: as soon as the light came on, a swirl of dancers would follow me as if I were some clothed Pied Piper, out the door and into the open world, into my buildings *with* windows.

There are five such clubs in Nashville, and I soon found myself shaking hands with each of the managers, who all agreed that, yes, working in seven-inch heels from early evening to three in the morning might merit a weekly, home-cooked meal. So communion—this time the traveling, hallowed practice of breaking bread together—became the thing I carried into the buildings without windows, accompanied by several women friends who echoed that concrete-splitting question: What goes on . . . no really, what goes on in there?

And as *there* turned into *here*, which often happens, I think, when we follow our most earnest of questions, a new plea emerged. Or perhaps it wasn't new. Perhaps it was old and inherited, sleeping all those years, lounging undisturbed in my buildings with windows, the plea: *Don't take my Jesus away.* I learned the difference between asking a question and pleading a question, *What goes on . . . no really, what goes on in there?* and between planting my feet, shaking my fist, and plain groveling: *Don't take my Jesus away.* But I felt it happening, every encounter turning the lights on in me.

Till one evening a dancer named Ashton asked if I thought Jesus was insecure.

Insecure? Jesus? No. If Jesus were sovereign over *my* insecurity, how could Jesus be insecure? *Don't take my Jesus away.*

"But when he's in the garden and he's sweating blood, petrified for what he must do"—Jesus prays, "Father, if you are willing, remove

this cup from me; yet, not my will but yours be done" (Luke 22:41)—
"maybe there's no point in asking because he knows he'll do it, but
he asks anyway. Or even more so, hanging from a cross the last words
we hear are *why—why have you forsaken me?*" Ashton's words stirred
with passion.

I remember it being spring. I remember eating cut strawberries,
the room lit by neon lights preying on anyone who walked through
the door. I remember the music being loud and the silence being
louder. Ashton gave me room to speak, like a teacher gives a student
coming into her own. But I had nothing to say.

"Don't you see, Betsy? Jesus *was* insecure. But how beautiful is it
to know that he was that *human* with us?" And then the DJ called her
stage name, a different name than the one she gave me, and he called
it to the whole room. She rose to dance. It was her last night at the
club, and I never saw her again.

I don't know which word is more daring—*why* or *forsaken*—but
it was as if I were hearing both for the first time, as if I were asking
God both for the first time. A moment some call spiritual initiation—
a moment when "evangelism" was not scoffed but redefined. Gently,
she took my Jesus away. And the faith I frantically gripped collapsed
like a house of cards because this woman told me Jesus was human.
And no one in my buildings with windows had bothered to tell me.

Popular-culture feminism generally portrays stripping as empowerment: a woman seizing agency over her *own* body, exposing her *own*
skin, moving to her *own* choreography—is this not liberating? Is this
not essentially what feminism fights for? Doing theology from the
strip club, however, exposes realities beyond clothes coming off, the
undergirding patriarchy that proves to manipulate and oppress dancers.

The 1960s pornography surge reshaped the industry.[1] Both
"mom-and-pop" establishments and burlesque-like entertainment,
which buoyed striptease successfully throughout the 1940s and

---

[1] Sheila Jeffreys, "Keeping Women Down and Out: The Strip Club Boom and the
Reinforcement of Male Dominance," *Signs* 34, no. 1 (Autumn 2008): 151–73.

1950s, dimmed in comparison to Hugh Hefner's Playboy Club, debuting in 1960.[2] Before pornography's outbreak, a dancer's central concern was how much skin to expose, but with pornography, *touch* cleaved to customers' expectations.[3] Indeed, as finances flooded in, leading pornography investors (typically rich, white males) became groundbreakers for a new era of striptease, launching spaces that ensured its "commodities" kept pace with pornography's influence.[4] Therefore, because clubs could not survive the pornography wave while featuring only striptease, lap dances became standard by 1970, integrating the privacy of touch and intimacy with a stranger that pornography offered, but in a commercial sphere, a room dubbed the VIP room.[5]

Most distressing, because privileged males were steering female sexual commodity (or how women should sexually behave), a toxic, gendered hierarchy manifested in clubs.[6] Although dancers were once paid an hourly wage, shortly after the standardization of lap dances, "stage fees" became normative, which require dancers to pay management for the privilege of dancing, forcing dancers to make a living in the VIP room. It is a dancer's responsibility to hook a private dance; thus, if a night runs slow, she will likely return home with a *negative profit*, a dollar amount that she owes the club. She is not an employee but rather an individual agent renting a space for personal business. Meanwhile, as of 2008, the industry generated $15 billion per year, a number all but impossible under the earlier hourly wage/employee model.[7]

Moreover, because striptease has, from its genesis in burlesque, induced a tenacious discourse between "moralizing family values

---

[2] Kim Price-Glynn, *Strip Club: Gender, Power, and Sex Work* (New York: New York University Press, 2010), 31.

[3] Jeffreys, "Keeping Women Down and Out," 152.

[4] Ibid.

[5] Price-Glynn, *Strip Club*, 31; and Jeffreys.

[6] See Danielle R. Egan, "Eroticism, Commodification, and Gender: Exploring Exotic Dance in the United States," *Sexualities* 6, no. 1 (2003): 105–11, esp. 105–6; and Jeffreys, "Keeping Women Down and Out," 151-170.

[7] Ibid.

and free sexual expression," clubs are constantly isolated, appeasing the morally conscious while falling under the radar.[8] Secluded, these buildings without windows are frequent spaces for "violent negotiations," and hard drugs not only pass between management and customer but are also used to sedate dancers. In her research, Kelly Holsopple (who stripped for thirteen years), approaches clubs in Minneapolis and finds with every woman interviewed a motif of repetitive sexual assault and verbal abuse within the workspace, which backs her conclusion that "the common, underlying element in strip clubs is male customers, managers, staff, and owners using diverse methods of harassment, manipulation, exploitation, and abuse to control female strippers."[9] It is more than clothes coming off. It is Sisterhood bridled by patriarchy.

As persons of faith, before we can ever imagine feminist theology from the strip club, we have to walk in. We have to walk in not to flip the lights on, but to share in the dark, to build glass through the concrete, holding that "any principle of society that marginalizes one group of persons as less than fully human diminishes us all."[10] So, long as feminist theologians cannot see into the buildings without windows and dancers cannot see out, we recline at separate tables. Hence, we walk in, confronting the dichotomy between the "clothed" bodies and the "exposed" bodies of women, *choosing* to commune. From bodies clothed and exposed, we call out bodily oppression. In one chorus, we struggle toward the unraveling of patriarchy. Bringing glass to the buildings without windows fans a sisterhood to life, instilling that which "promotes the full humanity of women" and is thus "of the Holy . . . reflecting the true nature of things, the authentic message of redemption."[11]

---

[8] Egan, "Eroticism, Commodification, and Gender," 106.
[9] Kelly Holdapple, "Strip Club Testimony," The Freedom and Justice Center for Prostitution Resources. A Program for Volunteers of America Minnesota (1998): 1.
[10] Rosemary Radford Ruether. *Sexism and God-Talk: Toward a Feminist Theology* (Boston: Beacon, 1983), 25–26.
[11] Ibid., 19.

In her extended essay *A Room of One's Own*, Virginia Woolf claimed that for a female writer to embark upon the creative work of fiction, she must possess "a room of her own"; she must declare a freedom of space, even when it is not given to her.[12] The page always bears potential to become her canvas. Likewise, we contend that for the creative sisterhood within strip clubs to be sustained, the industry's cruel patriarchy must be dismantled. We name this from a room of our own; we name this from the table, a space set apart, "not simply in a physical sense, but rather a province of the mind," as Mary Daly put it[13]—a sacred space where bodies clothed and exposed deepen our understandings of womanhood.

My initial nudge toward strip clubs began to fade when I realized, six months in, that these spaces would not vanish, nor their conditions. The five clubs I frequent share several characteristics: hard drug abuse (including periods of using, withdrawal, and relapse), single motherhood (typically involving multiple children), chronic back pain, miscarriage, severed relationships with family, eating disorders, domestic abuse, childhood sexual violation, financial desperation, prostitution, depression, and, perhaps most obvious, relentless verbal and physical assault. *This* is what goes on . . . *really*— this is what goes on, not in *there*, but in *here*. Sharing in the *here*— bearing witness to and advocating for dancers amid injustice and trauma, and continuing to be invited into their narratives—is what keeps us returning.

*Here* where Ashton is. *Here* where a neon heel pierces the Nashville skyline, flickering both night and day. I wish I had begun my time in strip clubs as a feminist, that I could tell of its conviction huddling with us around the table, passed over inaugural casseroles and peach cobblers that we could barely scoop through the dark. But

---

[12] Virginia Woolf, *A Room of One's Own* (1929; repr., Adelaide, South Australia: University of Adelaide, 2014), chap. 1, last updated July 15, 2015, https://ebooks.adelaide.edu.au/w/woolf/virginia/w91r/.

[13] Mary Daly, "The Spiritual Revolution: Women's Liberation as Theological Re-education," in *Feminist Theological Ethics: A Reader*, ed. Lois K. Daly (1972; repr., Louisville, KY: Westminster John Know, 1994): 128.

the truth is, strip clubs *made* us feminists. Ashton made us feminists. The truth is, the narratives we joined—a prayer offered in a dressing room, a baby shower for a mother coming out of addiction, birthday cakes that drew entire staffs around tables, hands extended and hugs exchanged after customers bruised dancers with their words—all embodied feminist theology long before the books were read.

So now, from a room of our own, we crack the door, daring to conjure a club without sexism. The fight is not extinction, but transformation. We mediate resources because there are windows to see them. We commune at the table, one we will always fumble to find in the dark. We listen to and clutch the narratives that both brought and keep dancers in these clubs. And together we stitch a sisterhood of resiliency. It begins in the room, soon to stretch through the house.

Let's dance.

CHAPTER 13

# Art As Spiritual Revolution

Angela Yarber

E
mma Goldman is famously remembered for saying, "If I can't dance, I don't want to be part of your revolution."[1] Another prophetic feminist, Toni Cade Bambara, claimed that "the purpose of a writer is to make revolution irresistible."[2] And the bold artist Liza Lou added, "What art does is to coax us away from the mechanical and towards the miraculous."[3] Taken together with their bodies of work, these words move me, too, to create. As a dancer, I think of these feminist luminaries as guides, inspiring my artistic life. As I age and my body changes, I have retired from professional dancing and, along the way, discovered a new mode for spiritual and revolutionary expression: painting. As a scholar of art and religion, I have long known the power of images to evoke spiritual meaning, providing

_____

[1] Whether Goldman ever uttered this exact phrase remains a mystery, though it has been requoted so many times that it is attributed to her without question. In her autobiography, she described a time when she was scolded for dancing at a party, to which she responded, "I did not believe that a Cause which stood for a beautiful ideal, for anarchism, for release and freedom from conventions and prejudice, should demand the denial of life and joy. I insisted that our Cause could not expect me to become a nun and that the movement should not be turned into cloister. If it meant that, I did not want it" Goldman, *Living My Life* [New York: Knopf, 1931], 56).
[2] Toni Cade Bambara, *This Bridge Called My Back: Writings by Radical Women of Color*, ed. Cherríe Moraga and Gloria Anzaldúa (New York: Kitchen Table, Women of Color Press, 1981), viii.
[3] Jeanette Winterson, "Liza Lou," *Jeanette Winterson Blog*, April 10, 2006. http://www.jeanettewinterson.com/journalism/liza-lou/.

viewers with a visual entry point into faith. As an ordained queer woman, I have also long known that religious representations have long excluded anyone who looks and loves like me. So, I began an ongoing project of subverting this virtually all-male sainthood by painting Holy Women Icons, giving traditional iconography a folk-feminist twist. Now over fifty figures constitute my collection, with over half the icons dwelling in homes, galleries, and offices all over the world. Goddesses, biblical women, artists, dancers, and writers are canonized into sainthood by my brushstrokes.

*Miriam* by Angela Yarber, Walker Private Collections.

Once upon a time, when my teenage self was headed in the direction of Julliard, intent on a life as a performer, an encounter with a conservative church changed everything. "Dancing and performing bring glory to yourself rather than God," a trusted youth minister told me. Tucked into the darkest corners of my closet were my dance shoes (and my sexuality), and thrust into my hand was a Bible that said women may not be preachers. Bless the soul of a prophetic undergraduate professor of religion who affirmed that my long-trained passion for the arts could, indeed, coincide with my newfound faith. He introduced me to Miriam and myriad other biblical dancers; he gave me the "permission" I needed to reconcile my long-held feminism with my newly formed faith. I began to dance again.

Dancer. Prophet. Revolutionary. Miriam is the classic example of a revolutionary dancer caught in the grips of God's joy, celebrating liberation.[4] I learned of her story as I entered college, intent on piecing back together what a conservative version of Christianity had rent asunder: feminism, spirituality, and dance. I learned she was dubbed a prophet before her famous brother, Moses—before any man, actually. Miriam taught me that dance and faith do, indeed, go hand in hand. She taught me that women can become religious leaders, and revolutionary ones at that. In fact, it was no accident that the first person called a prophet in all of scripture was a dancing woman; dance holds prophetic and revolutionary power. When the version of Christianity that was handed to me at that conservative church taught me that my body was an object of shame, something to overcome, Miriam's dance taught me otherwise. Today, when popular culture objectifies women's bodies, Miriam's dance teaches me otherwise. When the long history of eating disorders that dwell within my body shames, scorns, and starves me, Miriam's dance teaches me otherwise.

In encountering Miriam, I began to acknowledge that my dancing body is beloved, holy, and worthwhile. I experienced a personal liberation, which is fitting since Miriam's dancing story in Exodus is the bulwark of liberation theology, teaching us that we are called to liberate the captives. "No one can end suffering except through dance," Alice Walker once claimed. "Hard times require furious dancing," one of her books reminds us.[5] And so does Miriam. In encoun-

---

[4] For more on Miriam, see the chapter on Miriam in Angela Yarber, *Dance in Scripture: How Biblical Dancers Can Revolutionize Worship Today* (Eugene, OR: Wipf and Stock, 2013).

[5] See Alice Walker, *Hard Times Require Furious Dancing* (Novato, CA: New World Library, 2013).

tering Miriam for the first time, I realized that dancing is, indeed, more than compatible with revolution.

When dancing alongside Miriam, it was ballet that guided my bleeding steps. I knew deep inside my disordered, broken, hungry body that my movement must be set free. Ballet destroyed my toes, hips, and self-esteem, and then I discovered modern dance. I learned that a great dance pioneer did some sacred feminist reconciling as well. I met Isadora.[6] Barefoot, clad in flowing garments, with a diaphanous scarf in hand, she stepped onto the stage

*Isadora Duncan* by Angela Yarber, Gamble Private Collection.

and rocked the world: the world of dance, the world of women, and the world of religion. She claimed, "I had come to…bring about a great renaissance of religion through the Dance, to bring the knowledge of the Beauty and Holiness of the human body."[7] Because ballet was the primary form of dance, Isadora Duncan knew she had to reconstruct dance to better honor the body. Ballet and Christianity imposed formal moral codes: bodies as weightless, ethereal, something to overcome; toes that relevé away from the earth and toward heaven; no falls. In the form of modern dance Duncan created, the body utilized natural movement, focusing on the solar plexus as the center of the body, movement based on breath, contraction and release, fall and recovery, asymmetry, and organic movement found in nature. Duncan stated,

---

6 For more on Duncan, see the chapter on Duncan in Angela Yarber, *Holy Women Icons* (Cleveland: Parson's Porch, 2014); Janet Roseman, *Dance Was Her Religion* (Prescott, AZ: Hohm, 2004); and Kimerer L. LaMothe, *Nietzsche's Dancers: Isadora Duncan, Martha Graham, and the Revaluation of Christian Values* (New York: Palgrave MacMillan, 2006).
7 Duncan quoted in ibid., chapter 4 epigraph.

"if my art is symbolic for any one thing, it is symbolic of the freedom of woman and her emancipation from the hidebound conventions that are the warp and woof of Puritanism."[8] My bleeding toes unbound, I, too, stepped onto the stage and studio floor, inspired by the likes of holy Isadora, a woman who tossed propriety to the wind, loved women and men unabashedly, and taught me that grace can be found outside of ballet, outside of the Christian tradition.

*Frida Kahlo* by Angela Yarber.

Among my feminist icons, one painter stands out as a revolutionary who emboldened me to live, love, and paint in the borderlands, evoking revolution with each canvas. Ever the revolutionary, Frida Kahlo insisted that she was born on July 7, 1910, which is three years and one day *later* than her birth certificate indicates.[9] Believing

---

[8] Isadora Duncan, *Isadora Speaks: Writings and Speeches of Isadora Duncan* (Chicago: Charles H. Kerr, 1994), 44.

[9] For more on Kahlo, see the chapter on Kahlo in Yarber, *Holy Women Icons*.

so deeply in the Mexican Revolution, Kahlo wanted her life to begin with the modern life of Mexico. Her life was filled with intense suffering. She suffered physically from a horrendous bus accident. She suffered emotionally from her passionate and often rage-filled relationships with both men and women, but primarily with esteemed muralist Diego Rivera. And she suffered spirituality as an activist fighting in the Mexican Revolution. In these ways, she emboldens us to power on, creating beauty in the midst of suffering, and seeking to create a world where all humanity is treated equally. Kahlo was a painting revolutionary who embodied what it means to passionately persevere. With bold colors and raw emotion, she painted anguish, rage, passion, beauty. I only wish I could do a fraction of the same.

And as I've aged out of professional dancing, painting has become my primary mode of both artistic and spiritual revolution. I draw upon Kahlo's notion of "painting her reality," which I liken to Toni Morrison's evocation of eschatological imagination in the sermon by Baby Suggs, holy, in *Beloved*: any grace we can have is grace we can imagine. We can create revolutionary new realities through art. In my work, I draw upon the notion of artist as prophet and the often-quoted Bertolt Brecht statement, "art is not a mirror held up to reality, but a hammer with which to shape it." Since the arts are not often promoted as valid forms of spiritual expression or revolutionary change, I think that manifesting, claiming, and using the arts as a tool for spiritual revolution is a step toward changing this. Inspired by the likes of Frida Kahlo and Georgia O'Keeffe, I give traditional iconography a folk-feminist twist with the Holy Women Icons Project.[10]

Miriam, Isadora, and Frida are some of the myriad revolutionaries who inspire and embolden me as an artist, clergywoman, and scholar. It is on their brave, dancing, daring, painting, prophesying shoulders that we all stand, intent on making the world a better and more beautiful place for all people. As a feminist who was told to believe a version of faith that belittled women and demonized

---

[10] For more on my Holy Women Icons Project, see ibid. or www.angelayarber.com.

queers, Miriam revolutionized my life. As a professional dancer whose toes have bled through my pointe shoes and whose body wasted away in ballet classes, I think of Duncan each time my bare feet step onto the dance floor. Modern dance revolutionized my life. As a lesbian who thought for so many years that marrying a man would be the only way I could be ordained, acceptable, holy, valid, I think of Duncan and Kahlo each time I step into the pulpit. Fluid sexuality revolutionized my life. As a queer feminist scholar of religion who seeks to reject, deconstruct, and revalue what has been used to oppress, marginalize, and violate, I think of all these intrepid women when I teach, write, and research. Their approaches to religion revolutionized my life.

Whether it is dancing, writing, or painting, the arts have revolutionary and subversive potential. And I'll be honest in admitting that I've often struggled, as a feminist artist and queer clergywoman, to claim the revolutionary power of my art making when there is protesting to do, policy to pass, legislation to overturn, systemic violence seeping through the pores of our patriarchal and capitalistic society, work to be done to change lives and do justice and make the world a better place. When I engage in this inner struggle, I cannot help but think of a conversation between Israeli folk dance founder Gurit Kadman and the director of the Histadrut, Avraham Levinson. In the midst of the horrors of the Holocaust, Kadman approached Levinson and proposed the need to celebrate and affirm the Jewish body by hosting a dance conference. He responded, "Have you all gone crazy? You want to hold a dance conference during times like these, during Hitler's time?" Kadman responded, "The Jewish people are never able to be joyful."[11] An activist and dancer, Kadman knew something that is easily forgotten: the prophetic power of the arts to evoke revolution. Like Kadman, Goldman, Bambara, and Lou, I, too, believe that the arts are a vital part of revolution.

---

[11] For more on Kadman's role in the creation of Israeli Folk Dance, see Angela Yarber, *Embodying the Feminine in the Dances of the World's Religions* (New York: Peter Lang, 2011).

Misunderstanding the arts as merely decorative or peripheral may obscure their role in feminism and religion. The goal of aesthetics is to create a more beautiful world, a world where everyone can be inspired and surrounded by beauty. Aesthetics, put most simply, is the study of beauty and sometimes the theology of beauty. Justice is attained not simply when the hungry are fed horrible processed food or when someone without a home is covered by a dank and rickety shelter. Rather, when all have equal access to what is beautiful, delicious, healthy, and inspiring, *then* justice has come. As artists, we have the ability to help create that just world. Often propelled by religion, feminist artists have been doing this for millennia.

From the prophetic dances of biblical women such as Miriam, to the status quo–shifting dances of modern dancers such as Isadora Duncan, women have danced their faith as a way to evoke an embodied revolution. From Frida Kahlo to my own folk feminist iconography, feminist artists have canonized the holy with prophetic brushstrokes, reminding us that the goal of justice is for everyone to be surrounded by beauty. It is these daring, dancing, painting revolutionary women who embolden and inspire me to do the same. Because it's not just paint on a canvas or dance on a stage. The Holy Women Icons Project isn't just a touring exhibition or book.[12] Rather, Holy Women Icons are an opportunity for those who have never seen themselves as holy to catch a glimpse of their own worth. Dancing and painting is an opportunity to express lament and rage, while also creating beauty. For me, the goal of justice is beauty, after all. Creating beauty is a revolutionary act. Creating art is a holy and revolutionary act.

Miriam, Isadora, and Frida have rocked my world. May a glimpse at their revolutionary stories galvanize you to dance, paint, rage, and change the world as well. Liberate. Subvert. Unbind. Hallow. Rage. Seek. Revolutionize. We owe it to them, to ourselves, and to the world.

---

[12] Yarber, *Holy Women Icons.*

CHAPTER 14

# Letting Go to Let God

Rabia Chaudry

*"La hawla wala quwatta illah billah"*:
"There is no might nor power except for that
which comes from God"
—Prophet Muhammad, Sahih al Bukhari

I t took, as it often does, reaching a point of no return, a point of
complete and utter helplessness, a rock-bottom darkness in
which I sat for months, to finally reach the absolute understanding
that I had power over nothing. The only way to go from there is to go,
in humility, to God.

It's not that I paid lip service to God before that; I grew up with
God in my ear, whether it was in the ferociously whispered rosaries
my mother continuously fingered, or the Qu'ran always playing in
our car, or the Islamic lectures and debates on VHS that we reveled in.
God was in my ear when my mother lectured us as kids that we
weren't given blessings without accountability. "God will ask you
what you did with your time, your education, your health, your
resources, your life, what you did for others with everything God gave
you," she said. Repeatedly. "God is closer to you than your jugular
vein. He tells us that in the Qu'ran. God is close to you, always with
you," she said. Also repeatedly.

Such maternal exhortations planted the awareness of our intimate relationship with God deep in my heart, even when I wasn't
paying much attention to God. My mother made sure that even if we
"forgot" about God, we couldn't forget that God never forgot about
us. It worked. God was in my ear when I went away to college and
didn't pray because my parents weren't there to tell me to, but felt a
persistent weight in my heart. God was in my ear the first time I went
to a club with friends from campus and sat frozen, numb from the
experience of watching people drink and gyrate with abandon, my
heart repeating apologies to God for not being in a spiritual study circle instead on that Friday night. He was always there, and I never
rejected him, but young adulthood is a time for forgetting old things
and testing new things, while maturity is a time for returning to the
things that make up your soul.

So, when I found my adult self up against a wall, stuck in a terrible and at times abusive marriage with a man I had fought my family
for, having just quit a job in the wake of 9/11 and a boss's bigoted
remarks about Muslims, with no savings, no assets, a four-year-old
daughter, and nowhere to go, I gave up trying to figure out what to
do. I gave up trying to make the decision of whether to stay in a
lonely, dead-end, degrading marriage or to leave and face a different
humiliation—the stigma of divorce, single motherhood, and financial
hardship. So I dispensed with the decision altogether and gave it to
God. "Let me know what You want me to do, make it clear, make it
easy." That was my prayer, every night, for many, many nights as
everyone in my extended in-laws' family slept.

Within two months, my sister-in-law came to me and said, "my
brother wants a divorce. Please leave the house by the end of the
month." It was during Ramadan, and I was a bit shell-shocked after
her pronouncements. She had asked me, smiling and cheerful after a
meal together to break our fast, to join her upstairs for a private chat.
This, I did not expect.

But it was my sign. God had responded to me. I began
preparing and was yet woefully unprepared for how the marriage
would eventually unravel within a couple of weeks, with the police

in our home and me leaving in the middle of the night with a few bundles of clothing, my degrees, and an ancient, monstrously large computer that I hauled up from our basement bedroom. But not my child. He would not let me take my daughter.

The police advised me, kindly, that it was best not to make a fuss about it. They couldn't force him to turn her over or make her come with me. There were ten other people in the house, all her father's family. If I didn't leave, they could do anything to me or say anything about me. They could hurt me, or they could lie and say I was hurting them. Grab a few things and go, said the nice young policeman. Go to court on Monday and petition for your daughter.

It was a Friday, a day when Muslims traditionally begin all new things with a *bismillah*, and that night I left alone, after first standing at the bottom of the stairs, calling out to my little girl, who stood at the top with her father's hand on her shoulder. She wouldn't come down; she couldn't. Her eyes were huge; she neither smiled nor frowned. She was four years old, in her pajamas, and she stared down at her mother, who stood disheveled, face streaked with tears and voice hoarse from crying. Then she was turned around by her father's hand and disappeared down the hallway.

I too turned around and walked out the door of my marital home for the last time. I did not have my daughter, but I had God with me.

I spent the next eight months fighting for custody of my daughter, and the following four years as a single parent. It was a "best of times, worst of times" situation; I found myself on social assistance, struggling to secure childcare, and unable to pass the bar exam for a number of years because properly taking the bar requires taking time off of work to study and money for a prep course, neither of which were possible for me. But I felt fortified in a way I had never felt before. Those final months, and my literal release from marriage, were proof that God heard and responded to me. That I could "let go and let God," as they say, and would be just fine. It was the ultimate personal liberation theology.

This was the part of my life in which God and faith became active forces, as active, real, dynamic, and tangible as a gale-force wind. It wasn't about relinquishing my own power to make choices or effect change. It was about knowing that even in the times I wasn't sure what choice to make, I could confide my anxieties in God, turn over the matter to God, and put one foot in front of the other with certainty.

It was when I really started believing in this saying of the Prophet Muhammad: "How amazing is the affair of the believer [person of faith]. There is good for him in everything and that quality is for no one but the believer. If good times come his way, he expresses gratitude to Allah and that is good for him, and if hardship comes his way, he endures it patiently and that is better for him" (Sahih Muslim, Hadith 2999). It was also when the seeds my mother had planted deep—the seeds of accountability and responsibility we owed God—bore fruit. I began taking a hard look at the state of the world, at the conditions of Muslims and our communities, I began studying Islam in a focused way, looking for answers to the questions America was asking about my religion. I began responding, through writing, speaking, and interfaith engagement, as a means of fulfilling my responsibility.

When I finally began practicing law, I ended up representing many dozens of battered immigrant women pro bono. These were women I connected with because of my own experience with domestic violence. I began doing grassroots organizational work with the Muslim community to help strengthen our identity and sense of purpose and belonging in this country. I began pointing out our community's failings when it came to gender equity, inclusion, and religious and intellectual honesty. I began thinking deeply about and addressing issues of civil rights, national security, the so-called war on terror, and Islamophobia because I realized how all of these were layers upon layers that resulted in terrible policies, a less safe world, more fearful people, less love, more violence.

What linked it all—the thread that ran through every bit of my work—was God in my ear. When doing community and social justice work, which is physically exhausting, emotionally draining, and has no financial incentive, you have to have a source of authority, support, and renewal. Faith is naturally that source for me. It doesn't let me rest. God demands more, always more. As long as we are witness to the evil in the world, we are obliged to respond. "Whosoever of you sees an evil action, he must change it with his hand. If he is not able to do so, then he must change it with his tongue. If he is not able to do so, then he must change it with his heart and this is the weakest (manifestation) of faith" (Prophet Muhammad, Sahih Muslim, Hadith 34).

But beyond being the hand at my back pushing me to work, faith has also been where I found my answers to questions of terrorism, sexism, racism, interfaith relations and obligations, and justice. A deep dive into Islamic tradition, scripture, and history yielded hundreds if not thousands of examples and exhortations to work for justice, of Muslim women who asserted themselves as scholars and warriors centuries ago, of Islam's social service and educational imperatives, and of the egalitarian and pluralistic principles of religious and minority inclusion, protection, and equity that were bedrocks of Muslim societies, once upon a time.

At a time and place in history where vast Muslim-majority regions are crashing and burning, and violent extremists have not only hijacked my religion but are also using it as a justification to kill and destroy others in the vilest of defamations of the sacred tradition, there is no safer and sounder place to retreat for fortification than the tradition itself. There is no better rebuttal to the ugliness that terrorists have wrought on the Muslim world than the very weapon they claim to wield: Islam. Their defeat is in knowing that the rest of us 1.6 billion faithful will not yield our tradition to them, that they have no place in it, and that they themselves are rejected and abhorred by it.

And in this part of the world, the demand on Muslims is different but still strenuous. Anti-Muslim bigotry is on the rise; indeed, it is now en vogue for political candidates to be publicly and vehemently Islamophobic, making such bigotry a campaign platform.

When confronted with a supporter about when the country could "get rid" of Muslims, 2016 presidential candidate Donald Trump welcomed the question and responded that his potential administration would look into such issues. Not long after, another presidential candidate, Ben Carson, made the statement that he would not advocate for a Muslim president because Islam is not compatible with the US Constitution. These are but two of dozens and dozens of examples in which high-profile public personalities, including media and policy leaders, demonize Muslims with impunity. They do not get fired. They do not lose their candidacies or constituencies. They are not shunned in the way we shun those who spew, for example, anti-Semitic remarks.

This is the ultimate rock and hard place between which Muslims in the West find themselves. The Muslim world is turned inside out due to our irresponsible war on terror while we live in a nation that is increasingly hostile to our faith. And through it all, we have to keep working, raising families, paying bills, taking care of our elderly, trying to make our communities better, and praying our children don't grow up feeling lost and unmoored in their identities because they don't seem to fit anywhere.

Which is why, ultimately, faith and God are so profoundly important to me and my work. God in my ear is a reminder that while we are called to work for a better world our entire lives, it is still all temporary. This test will pass and we will all return to God. We won't be fighting poverty, racism, misogyny, and evil. We won't have our identities and loyalties challenged. We will no longer not belong. So it's that world, the world beyond this one, the eternal life that we will spend with God that gives me hope and keeps me going. That this, too, shall pass—all of it. And when you think of it like that, it's all small potatoes, with nothing but peace on the other side.

CHAPTER 15

# Christ, the Cosmic Vagina: Fear, Power, and Connectedness in Feminist Religious Peacebuilding

Trelawney Grenfell-Muir

I am a peacebuilder. Sometimes, official-sounding institutions employ me in socially accepted roles such as professor, minister, or program director. Other times, the work I do doesn't fit neatly onto a CV or résumé. People just . . . come to me. I help women leave abusive partners. I brew, dispense, and advise herbal/holistic/alternative medicine and wellness. I mentor and educate about many different aspects of peace: nonviolent theology and spiritual wellness, nature connectedness and nature-deprivation disorder, nonviolent education and schooling, nonviolent parenting and self-care, self-acceptance and therapeutic techniques for emotional wellness, and a litany of justice issues. In another time and place, I would have been a local Wise Woman, someone to whom people come for advice and help in myriad ways. To our disconnected, fearful, violent culture, I am a highly sought out nobody.

Every religion and secular ideology has its own definition of "The Good"—the purpose and meaning of life, the ethical standards by which we should live, and the most effective means by which we can achieve our existential and ethical goals. Christian traditions tend to use the scriptural phrase "the Kingdom of God," which describes a realm that exists somehow both here and now and also in the future or some other dimension. Within this realm, The Good is completely realized and fulfilled.

I started out as a Wesleyan: John Wesley founded my United Methodist tradition. My family and churches rejected dogmatism and taught me to value the conversation more than the answer. From a very young age, I was also encouraged to explore mystical connection with ideas of divinity and the natural world. I remember my parents encouraging me to befriend trees, talk with them, sing songs to them, and engage the natural world as a way to communicate with God. Methodism believes the path to Truth is found in the tension among a "quadrilateral" of scripture, reason, experience, and tradition.[1] As I grew older, my training as a biologist and then theologian influenced my understanding of reason; seminary taught me to approach biblical scripture as an important set of stories that reveal how certain communities wrestled to define The Good. Personal experience taught me that non-Christian faith traditions and secular sources of wisdom also contain beautiful and crucial truths about The Good. Moreover, my understanding of divinity and sacredness included increasingly direct lived experiences. I expanded: I became a Wesleyan Christian Universalist Mystic.

My faith taught me, through the examples of Jesus and others, that all people equally embody the divine image and that the wellness of one is inextricably bound to the wellness of all. My family and churches emphasized feminism, racial equality, economic justice, and care for the natural world as important aspects of The Good. However, the older I grew the more my own reason and experience bumped up against the parts of my faith communities and wider society that contradicted these messages of interconnectivity and egalitarianism. My own definition of The Good contracted and expanded. I left behind liturgies, social norms, and conventions that detract from interconnected egalitarianism, and I embraced symbols and identities that nurture connective equality: I became a Wesleyan Christian Universalist Mystic Ecofeminist Neo-Pagan Neo-Druid.

---

[1] Albert C. Outler, *John Wesley* (New York: Oxford University Press, 1964), iv.

I no longer use the phrase "Kingdom of God." My understanding of The Good has moved beyond both monarchic hierarchies of power and predominantly male divine symbols. I sometimes say the "kindom of God/ess":[2] a realm of kinship and connectivity. Other times, I say "JustPeace, positive peace,"[3] or simply The Good. Christian communities that emphasize boundaries between "us" and "them" sometimes experience my rejection of the phrase "Kingdom of God" as a betrayal. I have what C. Daniel Batson calls a "Quest" approach to religiosity.[4] Quest folks are comfortable with change and mystery, and we value compassion and justice over doctrinal orthodoxy. In my experience, Quest folks, whether religious or atheist, have much in common with each other, across religious or nonreligious boundaries.[5]

I first learned about "out-group intolerance" from the story Jesus tells about The Good Samaritan (Luke 10:25–37): Jesus designates a person from a despised "out-group" as a model of compassionate inclusivity. Jesus also says that when seeds are planted on fertile ground, they will flourish (Matthew 13:3–9). Those stories shaped me from a very young age, both to define The Good as an inclusive, egalitarian realm, and also to feel responsible for spreading those ideals in the world.

As I have studied and worked with communities of faith, academics, politicians, and social justice movements, I have gradually realized that the work of nurturing individual and communal wellness rests on addressing two interrelated issues: fear and power. Only by healing those two factors can our world embody the deep, sustainable, harmonious peace at the heart of abundant life. My faith tradi-

---

[2] *God/ess* is Ruether's term for divine that is both genders, neither gender, and everything in-between.
[3] Johan Galtung, *Peace by Peaceful Means: Peace and Conflict, Development and Civilization* (London: Sage, 1996).
[4] Batson cited in Russell Powell and Steve Clarke, "Religion, Tolerance and Intolerance: Views from across the Disciplines," n.d., accessed February 12, 2017, http://www.philosophy.ox.ac.uk/data/assets/_pdf_file/0013/13504/Tolerance5_background_reading.pdf.
[5] Members of their own religious or ideological group.

tion gives me tools for this work, with which to build and grow the interconnectedness necessary for JustPeace.

More than any other factor, fear prevents people from building JustPeace, or The Good.[6] The same fear that causes the out-group intolerance that motivates so much violence also causes people to feel uncomfortable with change or mystery and to prioritize orthodoxy. Fear prevents people from achieving the internal peace necessary to build societal peace. Trauma expert Laurie Estey once said that all people have three basic fears: unworthiness, trust, and abandonment. I think the root fear of unworthiness creates the other two fears: if I am not worthy of love, then people will abandon me; thus, I cannot trust easily.

We see these fears at work in every "ism" in society—at their root, all out-group intolerances arise from the same basic fears. When people exhibit racism or sexism, they are expressing fear that they are not worthy of respect or love as individuals; rather, they must rely on their identification with the dominant social group in order to receive respect or love. In addition, when nondominant groups reject their own empowerment— for example, when women believe they and/or their children *should* take their husband's last name—they exhibit subconscious fear of the punishment of the dominant group (or punishment from other women acting as agents of the dominant group). Of course, some women may choose to take their husband's last name for empowering reasons, such as rejection of an abusive father. Taking a husband's name exhibits disempowerment when it comes from a place of wanting to abide by patriarchal social norms due to fear of challenging those norms.

Fear undergirds conflict genesis, escalation, maintenance, and relapse. When people cling to identity labels or external criteria (such as wealth or power) to feel important or secure, they tend to treat out-groups badly. Many peace efforts do not address the underlying fear that motivates people to blame out-groups for all their woes. No one can move beyond out-group intolerance until they move beyond the

---

[6] The Good could just as easily be referred to as "The Good/s" plural. The ultimate "Good" of each tradition is surely a diversely understood concept and varies across traditions.

basic fears that they are unworthy of respect or love, cannot trust them-selves or others to give them respect or love, and will be abandoned.

As a woman, my socialization includes far more permission to admit and examine my fears than our society grants to men. Society teaches men that fear reveals weakness and undermines their mas-culinity. Male fear represents failure to adhere to the qualities that maintain superiority and dominance. Therefore, paradoxically, in our society, women have more fear of danger but less fear . . . of fear. Thus, our society socializes women to examine our fears more hon-estly, which allows women an advantage in finding ways to release our fears and engage with life more securely.

Simultaneously, society teaches that women deserve less respect than men. This conditioning hinders women's efforts to feel worthy of respect or love. However, since sexism defines women's inferiority as group based rather than individual based, feminism can help overcome women's fear that we are unworthy of respect. Communities that promote equality and empowerment can help women feel worthy not *despite* being women but *because* they are women. Similarly, men are socialized to believe that they deserve more respect because they are men, not as individuals. Thus, femi-nism can help men release the fear that their worth depends on superiority over women and find individual self-respect.

As my work with clergy peacebuilders illustrates below, religions provide tremendous, powerful tools for peace precisely because they get to the heart of people's deepest fears and offer a way to replace fear with faith. Of course, religious traditions and communities also contain voices of fear and self-rejection. However, as repositories of human communities' most existential struggles with meaning and survival, religions contain wells of profound wisdom and courage.

John French and Bertram Raven explained the bases of social power and how they operate to influence people.[7] French and Raven

---

[7] John R. P. French Jr. and Bertram Raven, "The Bases of Social Power," in *Group Dynamics: Research and Theory*, ed. Dorwin Cartwright and Alvin Zander (New York: Row, Peterson and Company, 1960).

found that while people can use punishments and rewards to control others, such influence is limited. In contrast, referent (attractive/charismatic) power, legitimate power, and expert power can influence people with wide ranges of views and behaviors, last much longer, and persist when the powerful person is not around.[8] In my study of clergy peacebuilders, I have observed that effective pastoral work increases a clergyperson's referent power. For example, one clergy peacebuilder's compassionate approach gave him the referent power to influence excombatants' choices about violence and crime. Clergy peacebuilders who rely on their expertise, earned trust and legitimacy within communities, and ability to help people overcome fear and reach for a vision of a better world can significantly improve the level of civic engagement in a peace process. More than politicians, who must operate within inherently coercive and hierarchical power structures, clergy can help their communities desire peace, shape a sustainable peace, and implement a deeper and healthier peace.[9]

My research on clergy peacebuilders has revealed that clergy with very different theological approaches interpret their traditions through a lens that releases fear, embraces courage, and reduces outgroup intolerance.[10] The motivation to study clergy peacebuilders arose from my experience of Christianity as a powerful path toward inner and communal peace. One of the most important peacebuilding tasks for all religions today is to help people heal from their fears and wounds. People sometimes resist this idea because they do not want religion to lose its prophetic edge. However, healthy self-love does not include a narcissistic disregard for others or for the consequences of one's actions. Healthy self-love comes from connectedness: the understanding that love of self *is* love of neighbor *is* love of God/ess. One cannot separate love into parts, just as we truly are not

---

[8] Ibid., 618–20.
[9] Trelawney Grenfell-Muir, "The Door that Doesn't Close: The Methods and Effectiveness of Clergy Peacebuilders in Northern Ireland" (Phd diss., Boston University, 2014).
[10] Ibid.

separate from each other or from our divine Source. Healthy self-love accepts that everyone is worthy of love because we are all divine, in the divine image, and of infinite worth. When religions help people experience and perceive their own divinity—as part of the interconnected web of all creation—people gain the courage to face the parts of themselves that hold them back from the deepest, most abundant participation in The Good.

For the same reason that clergy peacebuilders have advantages over politicians, women peacebuilders have advantages over men: our culture socializes women to have greater proficiency in noncoercive types of power. However, these advantages do not come from any inherent moral superiority. In fact, powerful women tend to exploit their opponents' weaknesses more than men do, use power more offensively, and use punishing coercion more than men.[11] Furthermore, across cultures, women are just as aggressive as men—we simply use comparatively indirect forms of aggression.[12] However, women do have peacebuilding advantages as a result of our socialization. Our relative lack of access to coercive or reward power has caused women to gain proficiency in using other forms of power to achieve their goals—the very forms most needed to nourish and sustain deep peace. New forms of geopolitics recognize the power of grassroots activity, wherein people take responsibility for their own security, change the rules, choose a different game, and arrange their own bodies on maps in ways that have global and international consequences.[13] In addition, women often approach negotiations in a way that preserves a web of relationships and prioritizes interconnected justice and harmony.[14] Women also tend to apply a more

---

[11] Laura J. Kray and Leigh Thompson, "Gender Stereotypes and Negotiation Performance: An Examination of Theory and Research," *Research in Organizational Behavior* 26 (2005): 103–82.

[12] Douglas P. Fry, "Anthropological Perspectives on Aggression: Sex Differences and Cultural Variation," *Aggressive Behavior* 24 (1998): 81–95, esp. 83–86.

[13] Sara Koopman, "Alter-Geopolitics: Other Securities Are Happening," *Geoforum* 42, no. 3 (2011): 274–84.

[14] Carol Gilligan, "In a Different Voice," in *The Conflict and Culture Reader*, ed. P. K. Chew (New York: New York University Press, 2001).

comprehensive, mutually beneficial approach to negotiations, and agreements brokered by women tend to last longer.[15]

When a society rewards power imbalances, that society is doomed to conflict. Anita Taylor and Judi Beinstein Miller have written that power asymmetry both causes and sustains conflict because coercion destroys autonomy, which is a basic human need.[16] They note that a feminist power construct must avoid coercive and reward power and employ mutual empowerment. However, I have found that power asymmetry causes problems only when a community rewards that asymmetry. When societies reward power imbalance, the power imbalance will grow and spread, such that community members view power as a zero-sum commodity. People see power as external, something they must gain at the expense of others and protect from the encroachment of others. This imbalanced lens leads to more rigid in-group/out-group boundaries, more fear and uncertainty and violence.

My definition of The Good means the kind of kindom Jesus describes, in which all creation lives in a harmony of justice and inclusion. Jesus stories are filled with cautions against the love of money, power, possessions, and rigid boundaries. Like much of the world today, Jesus's community lived in a society structured to maintain the power and wealth in the top few percent of the population, while the vast majority lived in disempowered poverty. Jesus's sharp critiques of unjust wealth and power, and his many spiritual resources for inspiration, fuel and guide my passion to use my power in service of the kindom.

My journey has also involved a fair bit of trauma and grief, which has shaped my approach to ideas of fear, power, divinity, and healing. Trauma is stored in the body as well as the mind and spirit.

---

[15] K. Österman, K. Björkqvist, K. Lagerspetz, S. Landau, A. Fraczek, and C. Pastorelli, "Sex Differences in Styles of Conflict Resolution: A Developmental and Cross-Cultural Study with Data from Finland, Israel, Italy, and Poland," in *Cultural Variation in Conflict Resolution: Alternatives to Violence*, ed. D. P. Fry and K. Björkqvist (New York: Lawrence Erlbaum, 1997), 185–97.

[16] Anita Taylor and Judi Beinstein Miller, "The Necessity of Seeing Gender in Conflict," in Chew, *Conflict and Culture Reader*, 65–73.

As I have healed from tragic loss, sexual assault, and domestic violence, I have gained profound insights into the spiritual connectedness of mind-body, self-other, and all creation. When I was pregnant, I experienced a profound sense of oneness with my child, a oneness I knew would change and diminish over time. I realized that my mother had felt that way about me, her mother about her, right back to the first humans, through all the stages of evolution, and back to the beginning of life on our planet. I realized in a dramatically physical way that all humans, all life, and all creation truly are One.

To counter two millennia of androcentric Christianity, I promote feminine images and symbols of the Divine within my Christian tradition. In this way, "the last shall be first," until we achieve an egalitarian circle. Sophia-Christ is the One through whom we are born again/from above: the Eternal Wisdom is a birth canal. She baptizes us with the living waters of the womb, She brings us from dim limitation and obscurity to realize our divine potential of Light and new Life, and She is the bridge that eternally connects us with the Creator Source and All Creation. Sophia-Christ is the healing Way through which we can journey and find each step of our path toward Enlightenment and the fullness of spiritual and embodied Love!

Vaginas are amazingly powerful. As Eve Ensler has expressed in her work about violence against women, *The Vagina Monologues*, vaginas symbolize the liberation and empowerment of oppressed groups. The birth canal our society covers up as shameful, exploits as a commodity, violates through widespread sexual trafficking and rape, and uses as an insult in numerous slurs is also the Way of life for the entire human race. All are conceived through a vagina, and all newborns crowned by a vagina, whether it be labia or a cesarean incision. As Jesus says in Matt 21:42, quoting the psalmist, "the stone that the builders rejected has become the cornerstone; this was done by The Eternal: I AM THAT I AM CREATING/BECOMING,[17] and it is

---

[17] The Hebrew scriptures use the term *YHWH* to represent the Divine. English Bibles often translate YHWH as "The Lord," but its meaning is actually, "I Am," or "I Am that I Am," or "I Am What I Am," or "I Am What/That I Am Creating," or "I Am What/That I Am Becoming."

amazing in our eyes." The vagina is the rejected stone through which the Source of all Being flows to create new Life!

Through Eucharist, the divine placental blood of life is found in sharing a meal in a community of faith and love: wine/juice becomes lifeblood when people drink it together as they join in becoming resurrection, becoming Life for the world. Sophia-Christ continually connects us to our Source of rebirth when we gather in communities of Love. The Cosmic Vagina can provide yet another meaning—a portal through which women can experience a spiritual, emotional, and physical joy. As a symbol of incarnation, Sophia-Christ represents the oneness of physical, emotional, and spiritual existence, a oneness women can experience during life-giving, love-centered sexuality.

These ideas may seem foreign and offensive to some Christians. Society teaches us to think of vaginas, menstruation, and sexuality as taboo—shameful, dirty, or sinful. That diseased socialization is precisely why using these symbols can save us. Our culture's fear of vaginas symbolizes and reveals our deeper sickness of existential fear and diseased power structures. When we can freely celebrate Sophia-Christ as the Cosmic Vagina Savior, we will know we have found a Way of healing toward interconnected JustPeace.

The Christian tradition includes vast, innumerable resources for peacebuilding through overcoming fear. These tools can move people from fear to courage and from inner and communal violence to peace. These resources shaped and nourished my own passion for peacebuilding from a young age. I loved stories of Jesus overturning the tables of money changers who cheated poor people. I loved mystical sayings about the kindom of God/ess, which exists both within us and as a vision for us to build and strengthen. My faith has always given me courage to face my fears, engage in activism and advocacy, and reach out in healing compassion to a fearful and hurting world.

I find inner peace, and I find the courage and inspiration to spread communal peace, through engaging fear, power, and connectedness via the symbols and stories of the Christian faith. The power of the stories of Jesus lies in their mythological truth: love is stronger than hate, good is stronger than evil, and life is stronger than death. I choose to believe this Truth not because I see evidence of it in every particular situation. Rather, I choose to believe because when I engage with the idea that this Truth undergirds the essence of Creation, wellness manifests within and around me. My belief means that I commit to this Truth and create it with my choices and relationships. Or, I should say, through the blessing of Christ's vaginal connectedness, *we* birth it together.

CHAPTER 16

# Losing My Tribalism (but Not My Tribe); Gaining the World

Nurete Brenner

O ne of my most sparkling childhood memories is spending
the Sabbath dinner every Friday night at my grandma Eva's
house in Netanya, Israel, where I grew up. The dinner table would be
set to perfection, with china dishes for each guest and crystal wine-
glasses for the grown-ups. The silverware and glass reflected the iri-
descent light from the Sabbath candles in the gleaming candelabra at
the center of the table, and to my eyes, the glow meant that God was
truly with us. We would sing the traditional Shabbat songs and recite
the blessings, carefully following the many rules of my grandmother's
Orthodox Jewish household, which meant no electric lights, no writing, and no speaking between washing hands before dinner and
reciting the blessing over the challah. And the whole family would
stand and sing the traditional words of the kiddush, the blessing over
the wine: "For You chose us, and sanctified us, out of all nations, and
with love and intent You invested us with Your Holy Sabbath."

There was, however, a shadow underlying this weekly ritual: a
pretense, a deception. My parents, sisters, and I were not Orthodox,
but we were expected to maintain the fiction to our grandparents that
we kept the strict traditions. As a child, I did not question this dictate.
Only as an adult do I appreciate the complexities and implications of
this ploy. It taught me that the insularity of our peoplehood needed

to be protected, that there was a hierarchy in which the traditional was somehow privileged over the progressive; it taught me to conform to the community's expectations and also to accept a woman's place as the traditional *ba'alat bayit* or homemaker.

My journey into adulthood has been about outgrowing some of these lessons. In the sometimes complex ways our childhood forms us, that early deception helped turned me into a rebel, an underground revolutionary, a questioner, a skeptic, and even a feminist. These traits continue to inform my social activism, but the flip side of the lesson was that it took me until adulthood to learn to speak my truths out loud.

Years before I was born, my parents had both struggled with the shift in worldview from their strict Orthodox upbringing. Eventually, they both moved toward a more liberal view of Judaism, and toward a more egalitarian or progressive understanding of gender roles, which culminated in my father choosing to become a Reform rabbi and my mother choosing to become a social worker and feminist activist. But shards of their own childhood experiences remain, like splinters in the skin. I remember my father exclaiming in admiration when he discovered that a friend of mine knew how to *daven* (chant the traditional prayers) at the synagogue. We moved to Israel when I was nine years old, and my parents sent us to Orthodox schools. There were always lively conversations around the dinner table about social justice, moral issues, and the relations among the various streams of Judaism. We would also play the "who's a Jew" game about actors in Hollywood. (Did you know that Winona Ryder was born Winona Horowitz? And Melissa Gilbert of *Little House on the Prairie* is Jewish too?)

I grew up with the comfort of knowing I was part of a tribe, even if that tribe was split into factions. There was talk about how Jews must always take care of each other, and we all learned the often-repeated expression "All Jews are responsible for one another." There was very little talk about other faiths and other peoples; Christians and Muslims were the other at our dinner-table conversations.

The tension that my parents experienced in breaking away from Orthodoxy has echoes in my own journey. Mine is not a turning away from Orthodoxy but a repudiation of the insularity and tribalism that were so much a part of my upbringing. My journey out of the tribal confines to an acceptance of a more inclusive landscape began—perhaps paradoxically—with my Jewish liberal education, which emphasized "caring for the stranger." My family took seriously these words from the Torah: "For the Lord your God . . . shows no favor . . . but upholds the cause of the fatherless and the widow, and loves the stranger, providing him with food and clothing. You too must love the stranger, for you were strangers in the land of Egypt" (Deut 10:18–19).

The precept instructing us to love the stranger was abstract to me until the day I actively participated in and facilitated an Arab-Jewish dialogue group in Cleveland, Ohio. It was in the dialogue group that I was able to learn to fully embrace and love "the stranger." Despite having grown up in Netanya, a town just a few kilometers away from the Palestinian territories, I never knew any Arabs, never had any Arab friends, and had never even spoken to an Arab. In fact, the idea of speaking to an Arab made me nervous because I had absorbed the fear of Arabs as the other, which permeates Israeli culture. When I moved to Cleveland and discovered it to be home to the second-largest Palestinian community in the United States (after Detroit), it suddenly occurred to me that I could meet the other on neutral ground. So, together with a newfound Lebanese American friend, I formed a Jewish-Arab dialogue group on the campus of my university.

Thus a paradox was formed: my journey away from tribalism was rooted in my tradition and sprouted in my social activism, which in turn strengthened my Jewish perspective. The stranger is someone who is different, who is other, who is of a different tribe. However, through the dialogue group, my view of the stranger began to blur. In fact, the lines between in-group and out-group, between us and them, between stranger and family were suddenly as tenuous and shifting as sand dunes in the Sinai desert.

Preference for our own kin may be a biological imperative, but just as a mother can love her nonbiological children, so too can we learn to care for and have compassion for those who are not blood relations. As Jeremy Rifkin asserts in *The Empathic Civilization*:

> By extending the central nervous system of each individual
> and the society as a whole, communication revolutions
> provide an ever more inclusive playing field for empathy to
> mature and consciousness to expand . . . during the period
> of . . . agricultural civilizations . . . empathic sensitivity
> broadened from tribal blood ties to associational ties based
> on common religious affiliation. Jews came to empathize
> with Jews, Christians with Christians, Muslims with Mus-
> lims, etc. In the first industrial revolution characterized by
> print and ideological consciousness, empathic sensibility
> extended to national borders . . . In the second industrial
> revolution, characterized by electronic communication and
> psychological consciousness, individuals began to identify
> with like-minded others . . . Today, we are on the cusp of
> another historic convergence of energy and communica-
> tion—a third industrial revolution—that could extend
> empathic sensibility to the biosphere itself and all of life on
> Earth.[1]

Altruism only toward our "own" is a cultural concept. There is no limit to caring for others. Certainly, we cannot take on every cause—this would lead to what social workers call "caregiver burnout." However, we must have equal compassion for children under siege in Gaza, for the children terrorized by rocket fire in Sderot, for children suffering in Syria, and for refugee children risking their lives at sea. We can choose to have this compassion for all humans; it is a cultural construct to believe that only our own tribe and extended family are of importance to us.

When I first initiated the idea for the dialogue group, my orig-inal goal was to use the gathering as a platform to influence others to a more politically liberal "peace camp" viewpoint like my own. I

---

[1] Jeremy Rifkin, "The Empathetic Civilization: Rethinking Human Nature in the Biosphere Era," *Huffington Post*, March 18, 2010, http://www.huffingtonpost.com/jeremy-rifkin/the-empathic-civilization_b_416589.html.

fancied myself already liberal and tolerant and didn't expect per-sonally to undergo any changes. But I did. Instead of teaching oth-ers, as I had originally intended, I experienced a shift in myself. I had formerly been subject to a dichotomous worldview of "us" and "them." But within the crucible of the dialogue-encounter group, I found that my way of thinking expanded. The group itself took on a life of its own and within it, my own identity shifted to encompass a more inclusive "we." I was no longer just an Israeli American living in Cleveland; my identity became a member of the group itself. And the profound I–Thou discussions became a touch-point on how I wanted to conduct my life. Thus, by embracing the stranger and the other, I discovered that we were one.

This dialogue-group experience ignited in me a passion to study, facilitate, and participate in more such groups. I wanted to understand better the enlightening transformation that I had undergone, to dis-cover whether others had experienced the same, and if so, how to reach out and replicate the experience still further. Upon my return to Israel after nearly a decade in Cleveland, I discovered another layer of paradox: by meeting the stranger in my dialogue group experience, the stranger had become my family. I discovered I had now become a stranger to some members of my family because I no longer myopi-cally saw Jews and Arabs, Israelis and Palestinians as "us and them." By expanding myself, I had also distanced myself from the views of many of my compatriots. I found myself alienated from the Israeli mainstream and not fitting in with the tribalistic view that the popu-lar media transmitted. And I found myself exceedingly disturbed by the casual racism toward Arabs in Israeli society expressed even by some of the most liberal-minded of my friends.

The Torah takes it for granted that when Israel inhabits its land there will also be others—non-Israelites—who dwell there with them, and the Torah makes provisions for these others. The Book of Exodus states that you should not wrong a stranger ("ger"). "You shall not oppress a stranger for you know the feelings of the stranger" (Ex 23:9). The legal code in the Book of Leviticus dictates that when a stranger sojourns with you in your land, you shall do him no wrong.

"The stranger who resides with you shall be to you as one of your citizens; you shall love him as yourself" (Lev 19:33–34). How did modern-day Israel, the nation I grew up in and the country I served in its
military, move so far away from these precepts?

The reality is that prejudice against Arabs in Israel is blatant, fla-
grant, and unconcealed by veils of political correctness. There's no
attempt even to hide this ugliness. A friend, who is a prominent Arab
psychologist, recently related how returning to Israel from an overseas
conference, he hailed a taxi back home from the airport. The taxi driver told him proudly that he refuses to pick up drunks and Arabs in
his cab—grouping the two together without blinking. My friend
observed aloud with barely concealed irony that a drunk might be
easy enough to recognize, but how does the driver distinguish an
Arab from a Jew? The driver replied, "I can smell them." Needless to
say, the taxi driver's olfactory sense must have been malfunctioning
that day because he never suspected my friend, the psychologist pas-
senger, to be an Arab.

Last year, at my family's Passover seder at my home in Karkur,
we invited an Arab family from Akko whose daughters have grown
up in the Israeli Jewish school system. My friend's twelve-year-old
was excited to come to our seder because—as she told her mother—
this would be the first time she would get to see what a real home
seder looks like and not just the ones she had seen at school. Should
I be shocked to learn that despite the fact that she had twenty-nine
Jewish classmates and myriad Jewish neighbors, she had never been
invited to anyone's family seder? Most of my Jewish Israeli friends
were unsurprised by this. These and other stories, anecdotes, and
experiences increased my alienation in the years following my return
to Israel.

My return to Israel after nearly a decade spent in Cleveland
allowed me to continue my peacebuilding work, which felt to me like
a vocation. Through peacebuilding, I gained a new appreciation for
and was able to fully express my feminist outlook within a peacebuilding context. History has demonstrated that women, in both an
individual and group capacity, are extremely effective as peace-

builders. This is not to say that men cannot be peacemakers or that women are never violent but rather that the achievements of women in this capacity are often overlooked. However, the inequalities between men and women that still prevail in our societies keep women from reaching their full potential in creating a culture of peace. According to Biirgit Brock-Utne, "even though women frequently build the backbone of peace organizations, they are seldom given credit for their work. They are mostly made invisible in history books, which frequently are 'his-story' books, describing the development of violent conflicts or wars started by men."[2]

The capacity of women as peacemakers must be recognized and promoted in governments, nonprofit organizations, and international relations, as well as in the classroom. The United Nations has stated its support for the active engagement of women in the peace process in numerous official resolutions and declarations, and now it remains for the world to follow through. When represented in peacemaking, we see that women carry a positive and significant impact on peace; encouraging their participation increases the probability of violence ending within a year by 24 percent.[3]

In the case of the Middle East, resolving conflict is no longer a matter of respecting the other simply because it is the right thing to do. The ethical treatment of the stranger has become a matter of survival. Middle East peace talks have led nowhere; most Israelis want peace but continue to live in complacency because the Occupation does not affect them personally; the military industrial complex in Israel continues to make money off the backs of our young people (who are collectively traumatized by arresting children, while simultaneously traumatizing a whole new generation of young Palestinians) as we continue to educate them to the glory of militarism. A shift is needed—a shift in consciousness must occur in order for Israel to survive, for the Jewish people to rediscover their morality,

---

[2] Birgit Brock-Utne, "A Gender Perspective on Peace Education and the Work for Peace," *International Review of Education* 55, nos. 2–3 (May 2009): 205–20.
[3] Laurel Stone, "Can Women Make the World More Peaceful?" *The Guardian*, August 14, 2014.

and for peace to prevail. We must all lose our primitive sense of tribalism.

I still celebrate Shabbat dinner joyfully with my family and now
with my own children. I no longer pretend that I am anything but
what I am: a liberal Jew, a feminist, a social activist, a mother, a professional academic, and a homemaker. I am sure my children will
find their own ways to expand their journeys beyond my teachings,
and I hope they will discuss them with me around the sparkling
lights of the Shabbat candles at our dinner table to which I invite
friends from other faiths and other nations and other tribes. For we
have changed the words just slightly in the traditional prayer over the
wine. We now stand and recite: "For You chose us, and sanctified us,
ALONG WITH all nations, and with love and intent You invested us
with Your Holy Sabbath."

CHAPTER 17

# I Dream Myself a Revolutionary

Xochitl Alvizo

I dream myself a revolutionary—standing before the people, giving a rallying cry, leading us to radical change. This is how I imagine I would be if I lived during the women's liberation movement of the late 1960s and early 1970s: electric, contagious energy being spread among women, women taking to the streets, organizing creative actions, and demanding change. I dream myself a revolutionary standing in the middle of groundbreaking, transformative moments: sit-ins at the office of the male editor of the *Women's Home Journal*, where we demand the publication of content based not on limiting and sexist ideals of women's roles but that reflects women's diverse range of experiences and realities; lawsuits that break through barriers prohibiting women from public-sector jobs and from receiving promotions in available jobs; smashing through cultural taboos that forbid women from running in marathons, flying unaccompanied, or courageously reporting partner violence in the home. All of this happened at the same time, an explosion of protests and activism that not only engendered societal-wide changes but also inspired the burgeoning of women's writing, feminist journals, and the creation of new presses. I long to have been part of that radical time in women's history.

The women's liberation movement was led by those who knew firsthand the cries of injustice. They knew that the world had to change

135

from the ground up—knew that a *total* overturning was needed. I was born in 1973, however: just late enough to have missed this revolutionary moment in action. But from these revolutionary women, and some men, I have learned to attune to the revolutionary needs of today. I have come to know that revolutions also can and must start small and do not always require someone standing before the masses leading the charge. The revolutions of today, if they are to be peaceable and if their means are to be consistent with their ends, call for radical change that begins "in a small way, at one single place in the world," initiating the new and tangible thing for all to "come and see."[1]

Jeanne Audrey Powers once stated that "power belongs to those who stay to write the report."[2] Powers was one of the first women ordained in the United Methodist Church and remains an active advocate for ecumenism and inclusiveness in the church. She stalwartly works within the system to propel change from the inside, motivated by her awareness of the violence that church policies are actively inciting in people's lives. In contrast, Mary Daly, a post-Christian radical feminist philosopher convinced of the irredeemability of the church's sexism and misogyny, took the opportunity as the first woman invited to speak at Harvard Memorial Church to call all women and sympathetic men out of patriarchal religions and their institutions. She invited them to leave behind "the centuries of silence and darkness" these religions impose and to take their own place in the sun—literally leading a walkout of hundreds of people from Harvard Memorial Church.[3] Daly was convinced that people had to work

---

[1] My understanding of revolution is well captured in the words of theologian Gerhard Lohfink when he speaks of the revolution God initiated in Jesus as one that changes the world while preserving human freedom. See Gerhard Lohfink, *Does God Need the Church? Toward a Theology of the People of God* (Collegeville, MN: Liturgical, 1999), 27.

[2] Jeanne Audrey Powers, "Panel IV: Women and Clergy," Religion and the Feminist Movement Conference, Harvard Divinity School Women's Studies in Religion Program, 2002, conference video, minute 6:57, http://wsrp.hds.harvard.edu/news/past-conferences/religion-and-feminist-movement-conference-2002.

[3] The exodus from Harvard Memorial Church took place on November 14, 1971. Daly was the first woman invited to speak there in its 333-year history, an opportunity she used to lead a walkout. Mary Daly, "The Women's Movement: An Exodus Community," *Religious Education* 47 (September/October 1972): 327–33.

outside of oppressive systems, or on the boundary of them, in order to help create something altogether new. She did not support giving one's energies to oppressive institutions, even if it was to try to subvert or transform them. Convinced that the systems feed off that energy, she sought to live outside of them and help create "New Time/Space."⁴

Both of these women, with their differing approaches, inspire and compel me to act. The tug I feel from each creates a tension in me that moves me to consider the need both to leave behind oppressive aspects of my religion *and* to stay so as to dismantle them at their roots. The particular mode of action and the courage required by each have helped me understand two things: first, the revolution starts from the ground up, and second, it must be structural in scope. For me, these two components came together as I found myself part of a small community of people who founded a Pub Church in Boston, being imaginative and strategic as we created an organizational structure that would embody the vision we had for a liberative, life-affirming church.

Starting a Pub Church, or any church for that matter, was never a vision I had for myself, but was an act born out of my willingness to critically analyze the precise place where I was and to get involved in response. I was amid a group of friends with terrible church stories— stories of judgment, rejection, and exclusion—of negative experiences because of the misogyny, heterosexism, and homophobia embedded within the church, its community, symbols, and structures. But knowing church was supposed to be a signpost of the good news Jesus embodied in community with his friends and followers—of a new divine reality—we jumped in to experiment with the good news for ourselves, in our shared context, time, and place. We responded from where we were, from the ground up, and took our time building the vision together with our collective input taken into consideration.

---

⁴ Daly defined New Time/New Space as time and space that is "on the Boundary of patriarchal institutions" and provided real alternatives to the phallocratic order that stifles be-ing (participation in Ultimate/Intimate Reality), in *Websters' First New Intergalactic Wickedary of the English Language* (in cahoots with Jane Caputi) (1987; repr., New York: HarperSanFrancisco, 1994), W–W1.

There was nothing explosive or high profile about it; if anything, we proceeded with caution. We moved slowly and tentatively, as we explored ways of being church that countered the harmful outcomes of the all too typical patriarchal, hierarchical ways of church. We sought to replace these with new experiences born of our collective efforts, albeit experimental, to practice being a church "with a diversity of thoughts, stories, talents, hopes, and hurts," where all we bring is welcome.[5] We were inspired by the participatory and radical vision we saw embodied in Jesus as he lived and loved in community with those on the boundary of normative society—a vision still visible to us despite all our human distortion of it.[6] We knew we wouldn't do it perfectly, but in light of the very real harm we saw being done by the dominant models of church, or had experienced directly, we thought it was worth our best effort to form a participatory, feminist, democratic model of church in design, structure, leadership, symbol, and word. We saw the need to be church in New Time/Space for both ourselves and for those who might be seeking a community with/in which to practice a new way of living and relating.

Thus, I found myself staying in church. I did not exodus in the same way Daly did—though it is certainly a worthwhile consideration and a choice many friends have made that I wholeheartedly support. Instead, I have stayed to actively participate in church, still compelled by the good news of Christianity I see embodied in Jesus and his community. I do not stay uncritically, however. Pub Church is explicitly feminist, queer, and antiracist in its practices, structures, language,

---

[5] These are words taken from the welcome statement shared each week at Pub Church: "Welcome to the Pub Church! We are a church in a pub and the Spirit is with us. In this place, feel free to move about, help yourself to food and drink, and express yourself openly—We come together with a variety of thoughts, stories, talents, hopes, and hurts; all we bring is welcome. We pray that in coming together with all our differences and with Spirit, we participate in a new, divine reality. This is sacred space." The statement generally stays the same, with a subtle change of one or two words depending on who is facilitating the gathering on any given week.

[6] Many, though not all, who participated in the start of Pub Church, saw Jesus's vision as good. We were a mixed group of people, some of whom identified as Christian and some who did not—but all with enough of a shared commitment in striving for a most just and emancipatory embodiment of Christianity.

and decision making. It practices expansive language and symbols for the Divine; it creates its liturgies communally; it shares responsibilities for facilitating the weekly gatherings among the group; makes decisions as a collective; includes time for feedback and critical input about the gathering every week; practices communion in a diversity of ways, with a variety of liturgies depending on who is doing the facilitating; very intentionally deals with the accounting of its shared resources in the most transparent way possible; and makes space for people to shift roles and responsibilities based on interest and availability. We are a small quirky bunch that meets in the dingy back room of a pub and have done so since April 2008. The small group of people who gather as Pub Church very tangibly help create whatever it is that Pub Church ends up being—for better or for worse—keeping it alive, or not, for as long as we are willing.

Some Pub Church folks are fond of saying that we make Pub Church what it is—emphasizing that it is up to us to embody a divine new reality. This is what I have always loved about Pub Church: that it is a New Time/Space in which we intentionally practice embodying a new divine reality—one that we collectively construct. A little microcosm of what is and what can be—a liminal place on the boundary between hurt and violence, on the one side, and enacted hope and inspired possibility, on the other. It was born unexpectedly from the ground up because a group of us was willing to respond to the pain before us and attempt to tackle it structurally, at the root, drawing on the wisdom of a diverse community of often marginalized folks. It is not a revolution where one stands before the masses leading the charge. It is the revolution of individuals committed to digging deep within themselves to experiment with and embody together the transformation they desire for the world and to work to make it available for others to also "come and see."

I remember Daly once lamenting that feminists today were just not radical anymore—not the way they had been in the late 1960s and early 1970s. "Where is the revolution?" she asked. In the moment, I was at a loss for words; I lamented with her, myself having wished I had lived during the women's liberation movement. I was familiar with the cornucopia of feminist journals on her bookshelves documenting the groundswell of change and activism of that time. Later that evening, however, as I shared the conversation with my household, we realized that the groundswell of radical change had not died down. It was indeed still with us, but it had necessarily dissipated into a multitude of varied and contextualized forms. Daly had participated in a high-profile time of revolutionary change that played a critical role in exposing and breaking open the stranglehold of institutionalized sexism and misogyny in our society. But as it turns out, that particular revolution is ultimately just one of many revolutions still needed today.

We need a multitude of people actively working in community to effect material change for human liberation, which is what I eventually shared with Mary when I saw her again. I reported to her that the revolution does not only look one way. There are many sparks of change, many revolutionary movements, and their radicalness is entailed in strategically tackling the interlocking web of systemic and structural oppressions at their root. These revolutions are not as high profile as perhaps others have been; sometimes they are taking place in a dingy room at the back of a bar where a small group of riffraff gathers to heal and creatively, joyfully, counter the harm inflicted by church. Sometimes, it means staying just long enough to figure out the next move. In either case, it is deep, slow, communal work that embodies a turn toward new, life-giving possibilities. And it is good that someone stays to write the report—to spark imaginations so that others may likewise be inspired to be a new creation, to practice embodying a new divine reality, and thereby take their "own place in the sun."[7]

_____

[7] Daly ended her sermon at Harvard Memorial Church and invited the people to walk out with her by saying, "Our time has come. We will take our own place in the sun. We will leave behind the centuries of silence and darkness. Let us affirm our faith in ourselves and our will to transcendence by rising and walking out together" ("Women's Movement," 333).